But, I Never Met Sinatra

But, I Never Met Sinatra

Ron David

CARON PRESS
Rochester Hills, MI

Published by Caron Press
584 Ashley Circle
Rochester Hills, MI 48307

Publisher's Cataloguing-in-Publication Data
David, Ron.
" ... But, I never met Sinatra!" / author: Ron David. — Rochester Hills, MI : Caron Press,
2004.

p. ; cm.
0-9760903-0-9

1. David, Ron. 2. Television broadcasting—United States—History. 3. Television
broadcasting—Michigan—Detroit—History.4. Television personalities—United States—
Anecdotes. 5. Celebrities—United States—Anecdotes. 6. Television advertising—United
States—Anecdotes. 7. Television programs—United States—History. I. Title.

HE8700.8 .D38 2004   2004111544
384.55/4/0973—dc22   CIP

Book production and coordination by Jenkins Group, Inc. • www.bookpublishing.com
Interior design by Linda Powers • www.powersdesign.net
Cover design by Kelli Leader

Printed in the United States of America
08 07 06 05 04 • 5 4 3 2 1

Dedication

This book is dedicated to my sons, Nick, Neil and Derek.

And to my wonderful wife, Cari
who helped me come up with title for this book.
She has been
My inspiration
My lover
My confidant
My best friend
My reason for living
For over 25 years.

Contents

But, I Never Met Sinatra

He said, "Call me Jack!"

IT WAS AN OVERCAST Sunday in Beverly Hills. Rodeo Drive was like a ghost town. That's the way it was on most Sundays in Hollywood. The unions force production to shut down on weekends. On Saturdays, Rodeo Drive bustles with high-roller shoppers and tourists. But on Sundays, most of the glittering stars and production people stay in.

We were filming TV commercials for Big Boy Restaurants, and I went to dinner with the agency producer, a couple of production people and our director, **Bob Salin**. Bob was one of the top commercial directors. He had great taste and a wry sense of humor. Most of our Big Boy commercials were humorous, so Bob was a great choice as our director. He would later be executive producer for the blockbuster feature film *Star Wars…the Wrath of Kahn*, a project that would demand three years of his life.

We decided to have dinner at a well-known restaurant, Café Swiss, about a block from Rodeo Drive. As we entered Café Swiss, I noticed that **Jack Lemmon**, **Walter Matthau**, Walter's son, and a woman were seated at the number-one table. I was pleased to see them together. I had always admired their work separately and especially together. We were escorted to a table closer to the rear of the restaurant. I was seated so that I could still see their party at the front of the restaurant. Our party ordered a drink and our food and immediately fell into conversation. After a few minutes, I excused myself and went to the restroom. As I stood at the urinal, I looked to my left, and who should be relieving himself right next to me....**Jack Lemmon**!

I have never been accused of being bashful, so I said, "Mr. Lemmon, I'm happy to see that you and Walter are friends in real life." Lemmon said, "Oh yeah, Walter and I are dear friends." He continued, "We were all so worried about him. You know he just had bypass surgery and we didn't know how he would come out of it. Thank God, he's doing fine." Lemmon didn't stop there. He went on for at least five minutes, recounting every minute detail of Walter's ordeal. He then asked me what I did and why I was in Hollywood. I told him I was vice president of marketing for the Big Boy Restaurants in Michigan, and that we were filming commercials. Now, I had been a TV director earlier in my career, and what I said to him next really touched his go-button.

I said, "Jack (by now I was on a first name basis with him), I have enjoyed and marveled at your entire body of work. You are truly one of the finest actors of all time. But I must say that I believe your strongest performance was your TV role of *The Entertainer*." The original feature film starred **Sir Laurence Olivier** and was shown on the big silver screen. Jack said, "Well thank you, Ron, but why do you think that was my strongest performance?" I said, "You can take the most powerful film performance and when you play it through the little TV screen, as opposed to the big silver screen, you take away almost all of its punch." I went on, "The proof of the pudding is *Psycho*. I saw it in a theater and couldn't shower without locking the bathroom door for a month afterward! But when I later saw it on TV, it wasn't nearly as frightening." Jack smiled and said, "Yeah, I know what you mean." I continued, "The thing I want you to understand is that your performance was so powerful in *The Entertainer* that it completely overcame the diminutive TV screen and lost none of its punch!" Now Jack was beaming from ear to ear. He came over to me and gave me a big hug and said, "Ron, I felt that way, too! You have really made my day, thank you!" We talked a little more about the difference between acting for the big silver screen versus the confining TV screen. Then we went back to our tables in the restaurant.

When I returned to my table, someone asked me, "Where in hell have you been?" I said, "Well, believe it or not, I have been talking for the past twenty minutes or so to Jack Lemmon!" They all pooh-poohed me and said, "Dream on!" I let it drop and we fell back into conversation. After we finished dinner and headed for the door to leave the restaurant, I noticed that Jack and his party were still seated at their table. As I started out the door, much to my amazement, Jack jumped up and said, "Ron, oh Ron, I want to introduce you to my friend Walter!" Whereupon he led me back to their table and proceeded to introduce me to Walter Matthau, his son (who was the spitting image of Walter), and their lady friend (who was just that, a lady friend). My friends, who were frozen in rapt attention at the door, were flabbergasted. After saying goodbye to Jack, Walter, and the rest, I left the restaurant, beaming. Not only had I met two of my favorite actors, but I really felt I had had a meaningful conversation with one of the all-time greatest actors, who turned out to be one of the world's really nice guys!

It Could Have Been Fate!

I HAVE BEEN ACCUSED of being "starstruck," but it is not true. I have always admired and been interested in people who have talent. Not just the people who are considered "talent," but also the production people, who are so important and effective behind the scenes. They are the ones who make the "talent" look and sound good.

No, I am not "starstruck." But I was exposed to a lot of talented people at a very young age, and my interest in them only grew. My mother was "starstruck." She loved the movies and she usually took me with her to see them. Movie theaters were, up until the late 40s, the main source of entertainment for most people. You didn't go to see just one feature film. You usually saw a double feature! The double bill would change every Sunday and Wednesday. So our family, almost always, would go to the movies twice a week or more.

I recall a trip we took to California when I was about eight years old. We drove from Detroit. There were no superhighways in those days. We headed out Route 66 and went through every town and every stoplight from Detroit to Los Angeles. The trip took about a week, and what a trip it was! Everything from farmland to mountains to deserts. What a country America is! We have everything you can find anywhere in the world.

When we got to Los Angeles, we visited all the tourist sights, including the Farmer's Market, Olivero Street, Fisherman's Wharf, the Brown Derby Restaurant, and more. But through contacts my family had, we were also able to visit some of the Hollywood soundstages where feature film production was in progress. I had an autograph book my mother had bought me, and I worked hard at getting all the famous people we met to sign my book. I had that book just about filled up. But, as with many of my childhood possessions, the book disappeared somewhere along the way. My mother was in seventh heaven on that trip, and I believe I got bitten with the bug, too.

My father was a radio and TV personality. He worked in Detroit, New York, and Washington, D.C. and enjoyed a more than thirty-year career in the business. His parents, my grandparents, had been circus performers. My grandmother was a lion tamer and my grandfather was a musician with the circus.

Sadly, my mother and father had divorced when I was about three years old. She remarried, and her second husband had a brother who was very successful and very influential. He had a wife and three children. The children had been over-privileged. In fact, they were spoiled rotten! Perhaps because I had been raised with little privilege and appreciated every new experience, he took me under his wing. He was my uncle by marriage, but he treated me like a son! He took me, with his family, to light operas (unfortunately, there are no more light operas—the children of today don't know what they are missing) and he exposed me to pro football, hockey, basketball, and baseball. He even sponsored a hockey team I was on (the McMillan Midgets) and a basketball team, too. Sponsoring meant he paid for all of the uniforms and equipment. One summer, he rented the penthouse of the Essex Hotel, right on Central Park in New York City. He took me with him and his family for two weeks in this dream setting. While I was there, we saw live Broadway shows. The one I remember best was

Annie Get Your Gun, starring a very young Ethyl Merman and the handsome Howard Keel. We went horseback riding in Central Park. We went to only the finest restaurants. My uncle once spent an evening with Lucille Ball. The next day, he sent a bathtub full of roses to her hotel room. That's the kind of guy he was. He was very generous. During the years with my uncle and his family, I met and had dinner with Detroit Lions players as well as singers and dancers. I even met and had dinner with Jerry Lester, who became the first late-night TV variety show star on *Broadway Open House*. I didn't get to meet the irrepressible Dagmar (she was a stunning, buxom, blond bombshell who was probably the real reason *Broadway Open House* was a success).

But all of that ended when my mother divorced her second husband. I was in high school, in my senior year. I was trying to figure out what I was going to do with my life after high school. My grandfather (my mother's dad) had worked on the line at Dodge Main, making automobiles for Chrysler. He urged me to go to school at Chrysler and study to become a tool-and-die man. Since I saw no other options on the horizon, I went and took the test for this. Luckily, my father, whom I had not seen since I was five years old, called me and asked me to have lunch with him. He asked me what I wanted to do with my life. And I said, "I want to be in TV, just like you!" It was kind of surreal in that I really didn't know my father very well at that point in my life. (We would be much closer in time.)

Early the next week, my father called me and told me he had arranged an appointment for me to interview for a job at WXYZ-TV in Detroit. TV was only four years old in Detroit then (1952). He told me it was an entry-level job, but it was a foot in the door. He reminded me that he started at CKLW Radio sweeping the floors for carfare. I was thrilled! On the day of the interview—a beautiful, sunny June day—I put on my only suit and got ready to meet my future. It was a felt, tunnel-looped-belt, pegged-pant suit, and I had a ducktail haircut. (Hey, it was what high school kids did in the 50s!) I thought I looked spiffy. Little did I know what was to come.

I made sure I got downtown to the Mutual Building, where the WXYZ-TV general offices were, early. The Mutual Building faced Grand Circus Park, so I killed the extra time I had sitting on a park bench watching the pigeons. As the time of my interview grew near, a terrible thing happened. A pigeon crapped on the left shoulder of my suit! I was mortified! I walked to the corner, where there was a bar called "The Brass Rail." Now, I was seventeen, way under the drinking age, and I wasn't allowed into bars yet. But I had to do something! The bartender saw my predicament and allowed me to try to wash the bird crap off in the men's room. I bravely set off for my meeting with the high-powered TV executives sporting a huge wet spot on my left shoulder.

James Riddell was the general manager of WXYZ-TV and WXYZ Radio in Detroit. Both stations were owned and operated by the American Broadcasting Company. ABC was the new kid on the block in network TV. WXYZ-TV had been so successful that it was literally supporting the ABC Television Network. James Riddel's secretary escorted me into his office. He was a well-groomed, graying, and friendly-looking man. He invited me to sit down, and we began the interview. He took a look at my flannel suit with the huge wet spot on the shoulder, and I'm sure the ducktail haircut didn't go unnoticed either. Well, the interview didn't last very long. Jim said, "Ron, I want you to talk to our station manager, John Pival. He'll talk to you more about the job." Riddell picked up the phone and called Pival. He said, "John, I'm bringing a young fellow into your office. He is looking to go to work for us." Jim escorted me into John Pival's office, gave John a kind of knowing look, and left.

John Pival was a rather menacing man. He was built like a bull, balding, with a pencil mustache. He made some small talk with me. But, as had Jim Riddell, he sized me up in a minute. (Me, with my "zoot suit" and ducktail haircut.) His next statement floored me. He said, "Ron, it is nice meeting you, but you must have been misinformed. We don't have a job opening here at the station, sorry!" I mumbled something and I left his office, quickly.

The bus ride home was horrible. I felt crushed and very disappointed. The bus ride gave me time to think. I knew there was a job available. My dad told me there was. I also knew that it was my high school "uniform," the ducktail haircut, and flannel, pegged-pants suit that had queered the deal. So when I got home, I did one of the few really smart things I have ever done. I sat down and wrote notes to Jim Riddell and to John Pival. In the notes, I thanked them for their time and told them how nice it was to meet them. I told them how sorry I was that there was no job available at this time. I also let them know that I wanted to make broadcasting my life's work. I asked them to keep me in mind when something opened up. I mailed the notes, and then I waited.

Two days later, the phone rang. It was John Pival's office calling. The voice on the other end of the line was John Lee. John was production manager of WXYZ-TV. He told me that I was being hired as an ET (electrical transcription) man. He told me the pay was $25 dollars a-week and to report to Studio A, in the Maccabees Building, where the WXYZ-TV studios were located, on Sunday afternoon. I was to ask for the director on duty, who would put me to work. The notes had done the trick! Pival and Riddell were able to see past the "uniform." I was about to start my career in broadcasting. The only trouble is, I had no idea what an ET man did! I also didn't know how unbelievably fabulous the next few years of my life were going to be.

The Golden Years of "Live" Television!

WHEN WXYZ-TV IN DETROIT was getting ready to sign "on-the- air" in the late 40s, none of the top executives of WXYZ Radio wanted the assignment as general manager of the TV station. Most people in the broadcasting industry felt that television was just a "fad," a "flash in the pan," and would not last. But John Pival fought for the chance to head up the station. John had been a "bouncer" at the Fox Theatre in Detroit, back when it offered live stage shows before the movies were shown. He went into the Navy during the war years. When he got out of the service, he got his hands on one of the first wire recorders (the predecessor of audio tape). John ran around town capturing the sounds of streetcars, traffic, birds, and anything he could think of to record. He was hired by WXYZ Radio, who used his sound effects on the air, and he eventually moved into radio sales. John would go on to become one of the great, innovative general managers in television. He invented many types of programming that still remain today. He was big on remote broadcasts. And the joke was that John would do a remote to "watch two dogs screwing"!

Network television programming was scarce in the early 50s. WXYZ-TV only carried six hours of network shows a week, and half of that programming was fed by the DuMont Television Network. Local stations would sign on and sign off whenever they wanted. When they weren't presenting live programming, they would run a test pattern (with which viewers could tune their sets at home) and people would sit and watch the test pattern and listen to the music that was playing behind it. If you were lucky enough to have a TV set, it probably was a big box with a small screen. Neighbors and friends would crowd into your darkened living room to watch anything that came on the glowing "Cyclops-like" eye of the TV set.

Those of us in the television industry couldn't wait to get to work. It was exciting, challenging and almost addictive. In truth, we were inventing the most powerful communication force the world had ever known. Most exciting of all, it was "live." There was no videotape. There were few props or scenery and lighting was almost a mystery. There was often no rehearsal time. Much of the time, we would go on the air and "fly by the seat of our pants." If we made a mistake, everyone saw it. The adrenaline flowed and we all were caught up in the "magic" of live television. We didn't make much money and we didn't care. We were in on the ground floor of a wonderful and powerful new medium: television.

We produced a lot of live variety shows, featuring almost every recording artist in the business. Two of the top disc jockeys in radio, **Ed McKenzie** and **Mickey Shorr**, had weekly shows on the station. Remember, these were the days before the big "payola" scandal and recording artists would fly into Detroit to do the variety shows for a pittance. The exposure on TV in Detroit, which was then a key city for the record business, was important for every recording artist. As a result, I got to work with a cornucopia of America's top talent.

Here is just a partial list of the wonderful talent I worked with during those early days:

Chet Baker, Count Basie, Dave Brubeck, Barbara Carroll, Betty Clooney, Don Cornell, Walter Cronkite, Bobby Darin,

Fats Domino, Hugh Downs, Duke Ellington, Ella Fitzgerald, The Four Freshmen, Terry Gibbs, Dizzy Gillespie, Benny Goodman, Edie Gorme, Buddy Greco, Lionel Hampton, Bill Haley and The Comets, Gene Krupa, Peggy Lee, Julie London, Jimmy McPartland, Marianne McPartland, Hamish Menzies, Gerry Mulligan, Chet Baker, Oscar Peterson, Ruth Price, Johnny Ray, Soupy Sales, Rod Serling, George Shearing, Sarah Vaughan, Dinah Washington, Andy Williams, Teddy Wilson, Red Norvo, Johnny Desmond, Sammy Davis Jr., Jamie Farr, Don Shirley, Art Tatum, and **many, many more** that I cannot recall after so many years have passed. But the sad part is that we didn't record those wonderful performances. As I said, videotape had not been invented and "kinescope" recordings, which were less than optimum quality, were done sparingly. In addition to the well-known artists I have mentioned, our studios were filled with every kind of talent known to man. There were adagio dancers, ballroom dancers, ballet dancers, acrobats, jugglers, comedians, unknown singers and musicians and legions of other performers, all of whom were trying to make it in the business.

I mentioned that rehearsal time was very scarce in those days. Here's a good example of how it went.

The *Ed McKenzie Saturday Dance Party* was a two-hour "live" telecast. We had little time to rehearse or even to set sound levels or check lighting. When **Sammy Davis Jr.** appeared on the show, he walked in and I took him over to the band. He spoke to them for a couple of minutes and that was that. When Ed McKenzie introduced Sammy, he came out and sang, danced, did impressions and even did a part of his fabulous "Colt 45 Pistol "act." All of this with no rehearsal! He was great, and so was "live" TV. Today, a show like the Saturday Dance Party would be in rehearsal for weeks or even months.

Of course, "live" TV had its flaws. When you made a mistake in "live" TV, everyone saw it. One day, I was directing a show called *Robin and Ricky.* It took place in a diner. **Ricky the**

Clown (Irv Romig) was a local talent who always worked with a donkey. He insisted that his donkey had to be part of the show. So we put the donkey in a little room in the back part of the set that looked like a stall, complete with straw. I directed the show with only two cameras—a very hard thing to do with a lot of dialogue and action going on. I was cutting cameras between Robin and Ricky, who were talking to each other. When I would cut to Robin, we could see the donkey, in his stall, in the background of the shot. As I was cutting from one camera to the other, the donkey suddenly began to get an enormous erection! When I cut to Robin's camera, there it was ...and I had nowhere to go. I couldn't avoid seeing him when I cut to Robin. So all of our viewers saw it every time I cut to that camera. The worst part of it was that the show was aimed at kids. Believe it or not, no viewers called in to complain about what they saw. It was just another "wild and wacky" example of how exciting "live" television was with all of its flaws.

Soupy's On!

SOUPY SALES HAS BEEN known throughout the country for his zany antics. His huge bow tie, top hat, sweater, White Fang, Black Tooth, Pookie and the "Soupy Shuffle," as well as his trademarked pies in the face, have made him unique. He came to Detroit and WXYZ-TV in the early 1950s from Cleveland. His real name is Milton Supman and his home was originally in West Virginia. In Cleveland, he was known as "Soupy Heinz." Heinz soup was his sponsor. But John Pival changed his name to "Soupy Sales" when he came to Detroit.

The truth is that Soupy hadn't been very successful up to this point in his career. He didn't have a big wardrobe and he and his wife, Barbara, were forced to live in a duplex for the first couple of years in Detroit. He asked me to loan him $300 so he could pay for his furniture to be moved from Cleveland. But I was still an ET man and made very little money, so I had to say "no" to Soupy. But I, as well as everyone else at the station was very excited about Soupy's arrival.

We all did everything we could to help make Soupy and his *Noontime Comics* become a success. I was assigned to his show to spin the theme music and sound effects. His show was on five days a week. And again, there was little or no rehearsal time available for his or any other show. In an effort to make *Noontime Comics* as good as we could, we all went way above and beyond the call of duty. Two or three nights a week, Soupy's director, stage-manager Clyde Adler (who played White Fang, Black Tooth, and Pookie) and I met at Soupy's duplex to plan the skits and menus for the show. Remember, we were union members. We could have gotten into big trouble with the union for doing that, even though we were doing it voluntarily.

On more than one occasion I went with Soupy to a magic store in downtown Detroit. Soupy would pay $20 for a pamphlet of **Joe Miller** jokes. Joe Miller was an old vaudeville comic who was known for his "one-liner" jokes. Soupy would take one of the jokes and build an entire skit around it for his show. Not only did we have no rehearsal time, there was also no budget for writers. Soupy had to do it on his own. The amazing thing is…it worked! I could be wrong, but I don't think Soupy has ever hired a writer in his over 50-year career! I wonder what might have happened if he had employed good writers throughout his career?

Soupy's show was good enough to gain the attention of the ABC-TV brass in New York. For a couple of years, when the very popular network show **Kukla, Fran and Ollie** went on vacation, Soupy and his gang were asked to fill in. We produced the show for the network in Detroit. Jello sponsored the show. Soupy didn't get his own network show right away. But I'm sure the ABC-TV brass earmarked him for one as a result of his "fill-in" success.

A couple of years later, I had been promoted from ET man to stage manager and then to producer-director. I was assigned to direct Soupy's nighttime show, **Soupy's On**, which aired at 11 p.m., five nights a week. My schedule called for me to direct a 15-minute weathercast, followed by a 15-minute talk show, followed by **Soupy's On**, followed by a reenactment show, **Night Court**. These were all "live" shows, with no rehearsal! I would sit down in the control room at 10:30 p.m. and direct four "live" shows, back-to-back, and not leave my chair until 12:15 a.m.! The pressure was immense. But that's the way it was—it worked, and we loved doing it.

Soupy would soon move on to Los Angeles and the ABC-TV network. His show was an instant success. Top stars like **Burt Lancaster**, **Frank Sinatra** and many others fought to be on Soupy's show and take a pie in the face. It was amazing! Later, Soupy moved on to New York, where he did an early-morning TV show for kids.

Fast-forward to the late 1960s. I was now vice president of marketing for the Big Boy Restaurants, in Michigan. We offered gift-certificate books to be given as "stocking stuffers" at Christmas time. Every year, we would bring Soupy in from New York to do a 30-second TV commercial promoting the gift books. In each commercial, Soupy would be looking for Santa. And also in each commercial, Soupy would get hit in the face with pie in a hilarious way. As a member of the Big Boy National Ad Committee, I had convinced several market-ing directors of Big Boy chains in other parts of the country to pay Soupy to do versions of the commercial for their market-ing areas. Soupy made big money for doing a commercial that would only run on TV for ten days before Christmas.

One year, during the summer, Soupy was in Detroit and I was asked to join him for lunch. It was good to see him. I told Soupy, confidentially, that the last gift book commercial he had done for us was so good that I planned to run it again that year. I told him we would send him a check for $10,000 for the right to use the commercial again. He didn't even pause. He said, "Oh no, Ron...that's not enough money! I'm worth a lot more money now!" I said, "But Soupy, all you have to do is go to the mailbox and take out a check for ten grand!" He said, "Sorry, Ron...but I have to get more if you want to run the commercial!"

I thought back to those early days, when I first met Soupy. He didn't have a pot to pee in then. And I was one of the people who worked so hard to make him a success. So as calmly as I could, I said, "Soupy, I hear you. And I want you to know that we won't run last year's commercial. In fact, we won't be running or producing any more gift book commercials with you...period! I'll burn in hell before I'll ever do another commercial with you!" And that was that.

A couple of years ago, my wife, Cari, and I were having dinner with some friends at a restaurant in Detroit. Soupy came into the restaurant with an "entourage" and saw me sitting at the table with my party. He came over and greeted me like a "long-lost cousin." I guess he had forgotten what happened at our last meeting. I was cordial to him, but I hadn't forgotten what happened...and I won't!

The Clooney Clan!

WHEN BETTY CLOONEY CAME to Detroit to do a half-hour TV show at WXYZ-TV, she brought her mother, Francis, brother Nick, younger sister Gail and her uncle George Gilfoyle, who was also her manager. She rented a house in Northwest Detroit to house the Clooney "clan".

Betty's sister **Rosemary Clooney** was already a major recording artist and movie star. The sisters had been an act in the early days. They sang with the **Tony Pastor Band**. They traveled all over the country in a bus. Betty told me some of the horror stories of traveling with a band. She said, "Ron, it was tough! But it was a great way to hone our craft." Rosemary sang melody with the band and Betty sang harmony. As a result, Rosemary's voice became stronger than Betty's voice. Don't get me wrong. Betty sang very well and had a lot of talent.

Uncle George got Betty the shot at a TV show in Detroit. By the way, Betty's nephew, **George Clooney**, was named after good old Uncle **George Gilfoyle**. I was assigned to the show as stage manager. Betty was the star of the show and we wrote little "skits" designed to lead her into her songs. Occasionally, Betty would ask me to act with her in one of the skits on the show. I was delighted to do so, although I had to join the American Federation of Radio and Television Artists union and pay dues. Being "on camera" and doing lines was great fun and the extra money didn't hurt either. Betty was a warm, loving, delightful person. She made it easy to work with her on the show.

I was invited to her house often. In fact, I hung around with Betty and her brother Nick a lot. The Clooneys are from Maysville, Kentucky. Horse country. So when they invited me to go with them to the Detroit Race Course on a rainy Saturday afternoon, I was convinced I would make a killing betting on the horses with their direction. They told me that some horses are good "mudders." A mudder is a horse that races well on a muddy track. So I didn't let the rain deter me from betting. I bet on six races, won three of them and lost money! That cured me from ever wanting to bet on the ponies again.

One day, Betty and Nick invited me to join them at a movie matinee. We saw *Shane*, starring **Alan Ladd** and **Jack Palance**. *Shane* was the first western movie filmed in "Cinemascope" and "stereophonic sound." We weren't ready for what happened. When Jack Palance shot the sheepherder and sent him flying into the muddy street, we jumped out of our seats. The sound of that Colt 45 shooting was unlike anything we had ever heard. Audiences are used to it now, but it was overpowering then.

Betty had been doing her show for several months and things were going well. The show was well received by Detroit viewers. We all loved working on the show and hoped it would never end. But Uncle George was hard at work trying to get Betty a network show. George had to fly to New York on a Friday to meet with CBS-TV executives. Betty had a chance to be on The **CBS Morning Show** with **Garry Moore**. It was the chance of a lifetime for Betty. The problem was that while George was in New York for the meeting, Betty had to be in Canton, Ohio, on Saturday for an all-day, outdoor performance. And although they had a car, none of them could drive it! That's right, Betty, Nick, Francis, Gail...none of them had a driver's license. So they asked me if I would go with them and drive the car. I said I would. We finished Betty's TV show at 11:30 p.m. and I met them at their house around midnight. We took off into the darkness, headed for Canton. We arrived at about four in the morning and checked into a hotel for about two or three hours' sleep. We had breakfast and drove out to the field, where they had a huge stage for Betty's performance. Actually, Betty did five or six performances that day and evening. Here I was, out in that fresh air and operating on little sleep. Betty's last show was over at around 11:30 p.m. We all got into the car—Betty, Nick, Francis, Gail and me—ready to head out into the darkness again to Detroit. Betty looked at me and saw that I was exhausted. She got out of the car and came back with one of the musicians. He had a small paper cup of water in one hand and a small pill in the other. He said, "Here, man, take this. It'll keep you awake until you get Betty home." So I took the pill...and boy, did it ever keep me awake! I couldn't have closed my eyes if I wanted to. I found out later that he had given me an "upper." It worked great. We sang songs for awhile, but eventually, all of my passengers conked out and went to sleep. I was fine until we got just outside of Toledo. Then the "upper" wore off. This time, I couldn't keep my eyes open! But we made it to Betty's house in one piece.

It was early Sunday morning when we arrived home. Uncle George was back from New York. He had to drive me home because I was so crashed, I couldn't drive myself home. He had good news for Betty and bad news for those of us who worked with Betty. George had signed the deal for Betty to be a regular on the **CBS Morning Show**.

It was great seeing Betty on the network. She worked well with Garry Moore. After doing the show for several months, Betty wanted to take a vacation. CBS brought in **Edie Adams**, who at the time was married to **Ernie Kovacs**, the comedian. Edie was beautiful and could not only sing, but also dance. The bad news is that Betty never came back to the *Morning Show*. Edie had taken her job...permanently! Betty was out.

I lost touch with her for many years—although I did meet Rosemary a couple of times when I was in Los Angeles shooting commercials. By this time, Rosemary had gotten as big as a house and wore muumuus instead of dresses. Betty had married the bandleader from the *Morning Show*. His name was **Pupi Campo**, and he now conducted the house band at **Caesar's Palace** in Las Vegas. He and Betty were living in Las Vegas and Betty had become a nurse. Once, when I was in Los Angeles, I called her in Las Vegas. I had been told that her health was not good. She had phlebitis, which is a very dangerous condition. We had a good long talk on the phone and recalled the "fun" days in Detroit. Unfortunately, one of the blood clots let loose a couple of months later and, as a result, Betty died.

Fast forward to the year 2000. I am now retired and a volunteer reader for Recording for the Blind and Dyslexic in Detroit. One of the volunteers and I were talking and she told me that her brother was an engineer at a radio station in Cincinnati, Ohio. She told me that he worked with **Nick Clooney**. Nick had gone into radio and was one of the top radio personalities in Cincinnati. I told this lady that I knew Nick very well. She said, "I don't believe it! I'll have my brother ask Nick Clooney if he knows you." I said, "I'll bet you a drink that Nick says he knows me!" About a week later, I came into the studio at Recording for the Blind and Dyslexic and the woman walked up to me and handed me a small bottle of champagne. There was a note attached to the bottle. She said, "I guess I was wrong. Not only did Nick say he knew you, but he said he remembered "those days in Detroit" and that he would love to see you again!"

I still haven't opened the bottle of champagne, and I reread the note from Nick every now and then. My wife and I pass through Cincinnati every March when we go to Florida for a month. I plan to call Nick and set up a lunch with him when we head south this year.

The Clooney clan lives on with Nick doing radio and TV. George Clooney is keeping the name in the national spotlight. He's a lucky guy to have a father like Nick—and even luckier to have had Betty as an aunt.

Eat, Sleep, and Breathe "Show Business"!

IT'S EASY TO GET completely immersed in what you are doing, especially if you love what you are doing. During my early years in television, I literally ate, slept and breathed "show business." I read every show business tabloid (*Variety, Billboard, Cash Box*) cover to cover, every week. I could tell you what movies were running, what their box office receipts were and who was appearing where, when, and at what club, anywhere in the United States.

I went to New York and Las Vegas regularly. One year, I took a two-week vacation to Las Vegas. While there, I saw almost every show on the strip. I saw *Guys and Dolls* with the original cast. One day at the **Dunes Hotel** pool, I sat and talked with the star of the show, **Robert Alda** (his son is **Alan Alda** of M.A.S.H. fame) and other members of the cast for hours. On another trip, I went to the **Sands Hotel** to visit with a friend of mine from Detroit, **Bobby Stevenson**. His jazz trio was the "house act" in the lounge of the Dunes Hotel. While we were talking, **Johnny Ray** ("Little White Cloud That Cried" and other songs) joined us and we talked. In those days (early 1950s), Vegas was the cheapest first-class vacation spot in the world. A room at any of the major hotels was only $5.00 per night. You could see a major show for $2.50 and you got two drinks to boot! The entire strip was only two miles long. At the airport end, you had the Dunes Hotel. At the far end, toward downtown Las Vegas, you had the **El Rancho Vegas** (which later burned down). The land all around the "strip" was desert. Today when you go to Las Vegas, you would think you are in Los Angeles. For my money, it has gotten too big. I don't enjoy it as much as those "good old days," before the world discovered it.

In Detroit, we had several first-class nightclubs that featured top artists. **Baker's Keyboard Lounge** (the original owner, Ernie Baker, died recently at the age of 91), the **Log Cabin** and many other clubs featured top recording artists. I spent a lot of time at Baker's Keyboard Lounge. Many of the performers I worked with at the TV station would appear there. I usually got a table near the bandstand. People like **George Shearing**, **Marianne McPartland**, **Don Shirley** and **Ruth Price** would join me at my table in between sets and we would talk.

In New York, I had a heyday on every visit. I would try to see at least one Broadway show every day I was there. There were tons of great nightspots, featuring big-name recording artists. One night, at the **Cameo**, where I had gone to see **Teddy Wilson** play, the great songwriter **Johnny Mercer** ("Ol' Buttermilk Sky" and many, many others) came in and sat at a table near mine. He was with another man and a stunning red-head, who was built like a two-ton truck. They ordered a drink. Then Johnny got up and took off his suit coat, revealing red suspenders. He put the coat on the back of his chair, sat down and put his feet on the table and proceeded to go to sleep. Only Johnny Mercer could have gotten away with that stunt!

One day, while we were preparing to do Ed McKenzie's *Saturday Dance Party*, a friend of mine, Tommy Sleschinger, who was a "promotion man" for several recording labels (Mercury, Kapp, and others) came into the studio with a young singer who was to appear on the show that day. Her name was **Ruth Price**. She sang jazz and had a new album titled, "My Name is Ruth Price, I sing!" Tommy introduced me to Ruth and then I went about my business, preparing for the show. After the show ended, Tommy came over to me and said, "Ron, what did you think of Ruth Price?" and I said, "I think she is cute and she sings great!" Tommy said, "She thinks you are cute, too, and I think if you asked her, she would go out with you." Well, I couldn't resist the opportunity to date a name recording artist. So I got her number at the hotel where she was staying from Tommy and I called her and she agreed to go out with me. We dated whenever she was in town and we kept in touch when she was back in New York.

I spent time with Ruth on every visit to New York. She was appearing on *The Tonight Show* which was the original show, starring host **Steve Allen**, with **Louis Nye**, **Andy Williams**, **Steve Lawrence and Edie Gorme**, **Don Knotts**, **Tom Poston**, **Bill Dana** and announcer **Gene Rayburn**. Ruth took me with her to the show, which was televised from the old Hudson Theatre. I got to stay backstage and watch her appearance on the show. I had worked with **Andy Williams** in Detroit, so we talked for awhile while Ruth was on.

One night when Ruth had a meeting, I went to the **Hickory House** to see jazz pianist **Don Shirley** and his trio. I knew Don from his Detroit TV appearances. Don joined me at my table in between sets. At the end of the evening, which in New York is 4 a.m., Don said, "Let's go somewhere else and get a nightcap!" I said, "Fine," and we left the Hickory House. What came next was very unexpected.

Don and I walked from the Hickory House to **Carnegie Hall**. I said, "Don, what are we doing here?" Don said, "I live here. I'm using the great conductor **Shostakovich's** apartment for the summer." We went into a dark hall and took an elevator to, I think, the ninth floor. The elevator door opened and we were in the most fantastic apartment I have ever seen.

It was huge! It had a very high ceiling with two or three levels of bedrooms and bathrooms. It also had a grand piano. Don poured drinks for the two of us and excused himself to "get comfortable." He came back quickly in a red satin robe and a white scarf. We talked for a long time. He played some songs on the grand piano for me. When he rejoined me where I was sitting on a couch, he said, "Ron, I am so unhappy! I trust you, and I want to tell you a story." I said, "Go ahead, Don. It will remain just between the two of us, I promise."

Don proceeded to go into a long tirade about a young male student he had, named Herbie. Don said he was in love with the student (yikes!) and that Herbie's father found out and he ended the lessons with Don. Don broke down in tears at this point. I was pretty shocked! I was pretty young myself and had little or no experience with gay men. I didn't want to seem unfeeling, but I was very uncomfortable and had to leave quickly. I made some excuse about an early morning meeting or something and I left.

The ride down in the elevator seemed to take forever. I was relieved to walk out into the early morning air and go back to my hotel. That was the last time I saw Don Shirley. He was a terrific jazz pianist. He had earned two doctorates by the time he was twenty-eight. He was a gentleman and a gentle person. I felt sorry for him.

Ruth Price and I were getting pretty hot and heavy with our relationship. But Ruth had "issues." She was often very moody and aloof. A lot of it had to do with her family and things that had happened when she was a little girl. She never really told me the root of her problems. After a while, we kind of drifted apart from each other. The romance was over. A couple of years later, I heard she had married a musician. She was a great talent and a good person. I hope she found happiness.

Remotes, Remotes, Remotes...
The Essence of "Live" TV

I MENTIONED EARLIER THAT WXYZ-TV did a lot of remote broadcasts. We would do remote telecasts of hockey, auto shows, bowling matches, wrestling, golf tournaments, hot-rod races and religious services. Remotes were challenging because our technical facilities were limited. Television is broadcast in a line of sight. It does not follow the curvature of the earth, the way AM radio does. We had to microwave our sound and picture back to our main studios, where our signal was reinterpreted and then sent out to our viewers. At the site of the remote, our pictures and sound were fed to a microwave "gun" that was aimed at a microwave "dish" on the building where our studios were located. If there were buildings, or even trees in the way of the microwave signal, the picture and sound would not get to the main studio. So remotes were tricky at best.

I was assigned to many remotes, including some network remotes. I was sent to Toledo, Ohio, to stage-manage **ABC's *Saturday Night Fights*. Dennis James** was the show's announcer. But my favorite remote assignment was the ***Prophet Jones*** telecast. Prophet Jones was an ordained minister, who, shall we say, was very colorful. His services originated at the Paradise Theater, an old movie theater in the heart of downtown Detroit. Prophet Jones wore a long evening gown with long gloves. His hair was done in a bun on the back of his head. And he wore a little pillbox hat. His "right-hand man" was Prince Timmy Rogers. He was dressed similarly to Prophet Jones. We would telecast his services "live" from the theater for one hour every Sunday evening. The services were also broadcast on CKLW Radio.

Often, when we would go on the air, Prophet Jones was not even in the theater yet. We trained the cameras on the audience (which was 50 percent black and 50 percent white) and on the organ and tambourine music that was being played onstage. The setting for the show was simple: some over-stuffed couches and chairs, with a throne for Prophet Jones to sit on. Finally, Prophet Jones and Prince Timmy Rogers would appear and the audience would go wild! Prophet Jones had a few "quirks" about him, one of which was that he never touched money. He carried his money in a brown paper bag. When he made a purchase, he would hand the bag to the clerk and say, "Take what you need and don't give me the change!"

Every week on the telecast, Prophet Jones would speak of how expensive being on TV and radio was for him. At that point, his "people" would bring out a huge canvas tarp and lay it on the front of the stage. He would ask the congregation to stand. He would then say, "If you want me to be able to continue spreading the word of God on TV and radio, I want you to come up to the stage and lay down a twenty-dollar bill. Then go out into the lobby and have a drink of water. I'll come out later and personally bless you!" The lobby was separated from the auditorium by glass and doors. When you were in the lobby, you could not hear what was going on in the auditorium. Quite a few people would go up to the stage, drop their twenty dollars and go out into the lobby. Once they were out there and the doors were closed, he would continue. "O.K., I realize that twenty dollars is a lot of money for some people. So I will accept ten dollars from each of you, so that I may continue spreading God's word." More people would go up and drop ten-dollar bills on the tarp and go out into the lobby for a drink of water, awaiting the Prophet's blessing. When the doors were closed on those people, he would then say, "I understand that many of you find it hard to give ten dollars... so I am going to accept five dollars from each of you, so that I may go on with God's work." Even more people would go up to the stage and drop five-dollar bills and go out to the lobby. Once the doors were closed on them (and by now, the people in the lobby were packed together like sardines!), he would stand up from his throne and say, in a loud and righteous voice, "I can't believe there are any people still standing in this audience! So I am offering you a final chance to help me in my holy work. I will accept three dollars from all who remain. One for the Father, one for the Son and one for the Holy Ghost!" With that, he cleared the auditorium! There would be a pile of greenbacks two feet high. And there was never anyone left in the audience to see his "people" fold up the tarp, with all the money in it, and take it away. The payoff was that he never would go out into the lobby to bless the people. He would just leave the theater. His congregation continued to go through this drill every Sunday night, with the same payoff!

Prophet Jones had a mansion on Boston Boulevard, which was a prestigious address. The mansion contained at least 16 grand pianos. He would conduct private sessions with individuals who wished his "insight"—for a "slight fee." One day, he gave a private session to an undercover cop. And when he made sexual advances to the cop, he was arrested and hauled off to jail on a morals charge. He left Detroit soon after that incident, never to be heard from again.

I was sometimes hired on my days off to work freelance, on closed-circuit, national telecasts that were broadcast from the Detroit area. A closed-circuit telecast is one that does not go out over the airwaves to your home. Instead, the picture and sound were sent via telephone lines to only the locations where they were to be shown, usually theaters, where a select group of people could be gathered to view the telecast.

I was hired by TNT (Theater Network Television, Inc.) to work as co-director on the national, closed-circuit telecast of the dedication of the **GM Technical Center** in Warren, Michigan. The Tech Center is an immense, sprawling series of buildings which contain scientific and testing equipment. The center is spread over many acres. We had "rigged" a van to contain a control room and we had two cameras on tripods mounted on top of the van. Our announcer for the two-hour "live" telecast was **Walter Cronkite**. Walter was sitting in the back of a Buick convertible, facing our cameras and holding a wireless mike. Our TV van followed Walter, in the Buick, around the grounds of the Tech Center as he described the various buildings and what they contained. After he made reference to a particular building, we would cut to film footage of the inside of the building, which had been shot earlier with Walter. Our truck, along with Walter in his Buick convertible, would then race to the next building to be described. This required split-second timing. We had to be ready at the next location before each film clip ran out.

When I showed up at the Tech Center for the assignment, I checked in with the co-director who was to handle the speeches that would be given after our tour of the buildings and grounds. He was **Cort Steen**, a New York director. He directed many network shows, one of which was *The Voice of Firestone*, on ABC-TV. When he saw how young I was (only 21), he looked over the big cigar in his mouth and said, "You think you can do it, kid?" I looked him straight in the eye and said, "You bet I can, Mr. Steen!" He smiled and said, "O.K., let's get on with it!" And that was that. The script, for my part of the telecast, called for a sleek, bat-winged, experimental car to drive up to the Buick containing Walter Cronkite. Guess who got out of the vehicle? **Harlow Curtis,** who was the chairman of General Motors at the time. He and Walter exchanged a few lines. Then he and Walter got into the experimental car and drove off to the grandstands where the speeches and the remainder of the telecast would take place.

On the morning of the "live" telecast....it snowed! Yes, it was May 10th! But this was Michigan. And it was snowing huge flakes, but they were not sticking to the ground. A man walked up to me and said, "Don't you think we should cancel the telecast?" I knew that there were thousands of GM executives and dealers sitting in theaters all across America, waiting for the telecast to begin. I said to the guy, "Why on earth would we want to cancel the telecast?" And he said, "We're afraid that Harlow Curtis will get too cold!" I was dumbstruck. I asked, "Did anyone consult with Mr. Curtis about canceling?" The guy said, "No." Without even another word, I turned and walked over to Harlow Curtis and said, "Excuse me, Mr. Curtis, but one of your people thinks we should cancel the telecast because you might get too cold." He gave me an incredulous look and said, "Don't be silly...on with the show!" The show did go on and it was a great success.

Color TV was just being introduced to the country. I was, again, hired to work on a telecast from **Greenfield Village**, in Dearborn, Michigan. We produced a piece that would be shown "live" on *The Today Show*, *Home* and *The Howdy Doody Show* on NBC-TV. That meant that we had to do the segment three times, once for each of the "live" cut-ins. The segment was fairly complicated. Our host was **Hugh Downs**. We had actors who were dressed in Early American clothes and were riding in horse-drawn carriages. They had dialogue lines, which had to be timed to be given at the exact moments when they were passing by trees, which had microphones hidden in them. We also did scenes in an old building, where Hugh Downs was located. We got the scenes for the segment rehearsed perfectly. But color TV was new and the color cameras were extremely sensitive to color and light. Color TV required a great deal more light than black-and-white TV. If you shot a book on a colored card, the camera might go crazy if the colors weren't compatible. So it was a hassle to make everything we shot look right. Hugh Downs, who by the way had worked in Detroit early in his career, was great through the whole, ugly mess. He talked to me about people and places that he had known when he was in Detroit. We got all three segments on and off the air without a hitch. It was an exciting assignment, because we were inventing a whole new medium all over again... color TV!

Fate Creates a Curve in the Road!

I DON'T KNOW IF YOU believe in fate. I'm not sure that I do either. However, I don't believe there are any accidents in life. Things happen because they are supposed to happen. It was no accident when the network decided that *The Martha Wright Show*, sponsored by Packard Motor Car Company, should be telecast "live" from our WXYZ-TV studios in Detroit, I was assigned to work on the show as assistant director. Martha was a singer of some note and her show aired weekly on ABC-TV. The network director was Cort Steen, the same guy I had worked with on the GM Tech Center telecast. The New York lighting director assigned to the show was a guy named Danny Franks.

Danny was a staff lighting director at ABC-TV in New York. When I met him, he had already won an **Emmy Award** for lighting the network special **"Art Carney Meets Peter and the Wolf."** A year later, Danny would win another Emmy Award for his lighting of **"Nanitchka,"** starring **Maria Schell.** Danny lived in New York with his wife, Ruth and his baby daughter Susan.

We rehearsed the Martha Wright show for two days. It was a luxury we never had with our local shows. During the two days, Danny and I got to know each other pretty well. We liked each other and Danny liked the way I worked. He said to me when the show was over, "Ron, I think you should be working at the network." My heart leapt. There was nothing in this world I would rather be doing than working for the ABC-TV network…in New York! At that time, New York was the TV production center for the world. Hollywood still didn't think TV would make it and therefore very little, if any, production originated from the West Coast. Danny went on to say, "When I get back to New York, I'm going to talk to Dick Briggs, who is head of network stage managers, about you." Although I was a full director-producer in Detroit, I really didn't expect to start as a director at the network level. I thanked Danny, and said, "Anything you can do to make this happen would be great."

A couple of weeks later, Danny called me from New York and said, "I spoke with Dick Briggs, and he wants you to come to New York for an interview. I will be with you at the meeting, so get here as fast as you can." I flew to New York the next day. Danny met me, and we went to the ABC-TV network offices to meet with Dick Briggs. The meeting went well. Danny substantiated my credentials, and Dick Briggs said, "Ron, we will have an opening for a stage manager's job in a couple of months. Go home, and I will be in touch soon. We look forward to having you aboard!" I was thrilled! I thanked Danny for his great work and went home to wait for word from New York. I had been a TV director since I was 20 years old. I don't know of anyone else who was directing TV at that young of an age. I was now 22 years old and ready and eager to make a move.

One day, while I was waiting to hear from New York, the phone rang in the control room where I was on the air, directing a local newscast. My mother was on the other end of the phone. She said, "What are you doing?" I said, "I'm on the air, mom, what is it?" She said, "Are you sitting down?" I said, "Yes." She went on to say, "You have a telegram from the United States government. The telegram starts out with 'Greetings'…" My God! I had been drafted!

I couldn't believe it. Drafted at age 22. I thought I was too old to be drafted, even though the Korean War was raging on at the time. Anyway, I had two weeks before I had to report to Fort Wayne in Detroit for my physical and subsequent processing into the United States Army. I was to take my basic training at Fort Leonard Wood in Missouri. After the shock wore off, I jumped into action. I called Danny Franks in New York and told him the bad news. He said, "Ron, I don't know if you know it, but the Army has a big facility at the old Paramount Studios in Long Island City, New York. They produce all of the Army's training and propaganda films there. I think they have television equipment, too. Let me look into it and I'll get back to you." Again, I thanked Danny for his help. Wouldn't that be great to be able to utilize my professional talents for the military? It sure would beat being in the infantry.

A couple of days later, Danny called from New York again and said, "Ron, I was right. They do have TV. The place is now called the Army Pictorial Center. They have huge soundstages. One of them even has a pool built into it for a movie that was made there years ago with **Charlie Chaplin**. I spoke to a Lieutenant Jorgensen. He is charge of personnel. He would like for you to come to the Pictorial Center for an interview. He wants me to be in the meeting too, to verify your civilian experience. Can you be here on Wednesday?" I said, "Danny, you're a lifesaver...I'll be there!"

The meeting with Lieutenant Jorgensen was great. He said, "There aren't many men out there with your experience in television. We have a new mobile unit. It is bigger than anything NBC, CBS, or ABC has at this time. You will be assigned to a 13-man crew as producer-director. It is a job designated for a first lieutenant, but we don't have any officers qualified to fill the position. When you get to Leonard Wood, call me and give me your Army serial number. I'll name request you, through the Pentagon, to come here after basic training." I was floating on air! If I had to serve my country, what better way than as a TV director!

When I arrived at Fort Leonard Wood, let's just say the Army didn't greet me like a long-lost friend. All they did was scream at us and they even shaved our heads. Basic training is "the great equalizer". They want to remove any and all individuality in every man. My platoon sergeant was a black man named Richard (Dickie) Wright. He was a tough, seasoned veteran who had seen it all. He polled each man in the platoon to find out what he had done in civilian life. When he found out I had been in television, we became fast friends. He even appointed me as "acting sergeant" for the platoon, which meant that I would wear "slip-on" sergeant stripes and help him train the troops. It sounded like good duty. But it meant that I had to march the troops, calling cadence, in all kinds of weather. It was November, and they called Fort Leonard Wood "Little Korea" because the climate there was similar to Korea...cold and penetratingly damp! I found, after we had settled in, that a guy I played football with in high school, George, had also been drafted and assigned to my company, although not my platoon. He and I hung around together in our free time, what little there was in basic training. After three weeks of constant harassment, we finally got a weekend pass. George and I decided we would take the train to St. Louis for the weekend. The train dumped us off in the seedy downtown area. George and I headed for the nearest bar. It was Friday night and the bar was "jumping." George and I were sitting at the bar with our drinks, shaved heads, and ill-fitting uniforms when I noticed a guy entering the bar. He had on a straw hat and he wore an open-necked shirt and pinstripe suit. His face was heavily pockmarked and he hadn't shaved. It was cold outside and he was dressed for summer. He made his way through the crowd and sat down next to me at the bar.

George and I paid little attention to the guy sitting next to me. We were busy "crying in our drinks" about how lousy the Army was. Suddenly, the guy butted into our conversation. "You guys have nothing to bitch about," he said. He went on,

"Give me your hand." He took my right hand and jammed it into his left thigh. There was a huge hole there. "Now that's something to bitch about," he said. "I got that in combat. In fact, I became a captain in combat, because everyone else was dead! You guys don't even have anyone shooting at you, so shut up about the Army!" I said, "Who asked you to butt in?" He kept on talking and asked us what we did in civilian life. I told him George was in retailing and that I was in television. He said he was sorry for being so blunt. He even bought us a drink. When things settled down, I asked him what he did for a living. He said, "I'm a writer. In fact, I'm on my way to New York. I think I've won an **Emmy Award** for a script I wrote called "**Requiem for a Heavyweight**." It was produced and aired on *Playhouse 90* on ABC-TV. I said, "If you're a writer, I'm Santa Claus!" He said, "No, really, I am a writer!" I said, "O.K., if you're a writer, tell me how you go about writing." He said, "Well, it is a little different. I think of an ending. Then, I get drunk. I start from the end of the story and I write...backwards...to the beginning." I was shocked! I knew that some writers did write from the end of the story to the beginning. It was a technique often used. I really didn't believe him, but I didn't say so. I asked him his name. He said, "My name is **Rod Serling**." We talked a little while longer and he excused himself, saying, "I have to catch my train to New York...see ya!"

George and I returned to Fort Leonard Wood on Sunday afternoon. That evening, we went to the company "day room," where we could watch television. The Emmy Awards telecast came on. When they came to the "Best Writing for a TV Drama" award, they announced... "The winner is Rod Serling, for "Requiem for a Heavyweight." The guy who came up to receive the award was dressed in a tuxedo and clean-shaven. But without a doubt, he was the guy that George and I had talked to in St. Louis. If you noticed, on the *Twilight Zone*, the camera stayed wide on Serling. After a couple of seasons and a lot of Hollywood "makeovers," the camera finally moved in closer on a much more handsome and smooth-skinned Rod Serling.

The final five weeks of basic training were cold and tough. As "acting sergeant" I was exempt from KP and guard duty. However, whenever the troops went out into the field, there I was, calling cadence and marching the troops. During the last week of basic training, I awoke during the night in a cold sweat, but I was burning up with fever. I was rushed to the base hospital. In the morning, I felt better. The doctor came by to see me and he told me that I had pneumonia. He told me I would be in the hospital for at least ten days. I panicked. I was supposed to leave for New York in a few days. What would happen now?

I decided to relax and get better. When I was released from the hospital, I returned to my company and was told that I had to wait for new orders. My company had moved on to wherever their orders took them. I spent the next week lounging in an orderly room in one of the barracks, playing solitaire, until I thought I would go crazy. Finally, a soldier came to my room and said, "Your new orders have come in. Report to the captain immediately." I ran down the stairs and reported to the office of Captain Montgomery, my command-ing officer. He gave me a queer look, almost a nasty look, and said, "Here are your new orders, David. It looks like you won't be going to New York after all. You're headed for Korea!" I reeled at the thought. Then I said, "Captain Montgomery, I request permission to go to Classification and Assignment. There has been a horrible mistake." Captain Montgomery said, "Permission denied!" I saluted the captain and headed straight for Classification and Assignment.

I barged through the door and found myself in front of a sergeant who had hash marks all the way up his sleeve. He had the stub of a cigar in his mouth and he was taken by surprise when I blurted out, "Sergeant, I need help!" He asked me what the problem was and I told him. He said, "Just a minute—I'll take a look and see what happened." It seemed like an eternity, but he finally came back. He said, "I know what happened. We have a "shavetail" here who hates his assignment. He also hates it when he sees guys getting orders for good duty. I'm sure he's the one who changed your orders. I'll take care of him, don't you worry. You were 'name requested' by the Pentagon. God Almighty couldn't change these orders. Go back to the orderly room and pack. I'll recut your orders for New York today. You'll be on your way tomorrow!"

I wanted to kiss the sergeant! I thanked him heartily and I turned and left the building. As I was walking back to the barracks, I saw Captain Montgomery approaching. He saw me leaving Classification and Assignment. I snapped to attention and saluted. He saluted back and said, "David, did you go to Classification and Assignment when I told you not to?" I said, "Yes sir!" He said, "Well, what did they say?" I said, "They told me I was right, there had been a mistake. I am going to New York, sir." He broke into a smile and said, "Good for you, David." Then he went on his way. Going to Classification and Assignment was probably the second smartest thing I ever did.

I finally arrived at the Army Pictorial Center. It was a huge place that took up an entire square city block. I found that I was to be assigned as producer-director for Field Unit #1. The unit included a 13-man crew and a tractor-trailer, which contained a control room, lights, backdrops, and other staging materials. There was also a staff car, a two-and-a-half ton maintenance truck, and assorted other vehicles. Our commanding officer was a guy named Lieutenant Bud Myers. He had been in TV in civilian life, but as CO, he was not allowed to act as director for the unit. The job I had should have been filled by at least a first lieutenant, and here I was, a "slick sleeve" private! I familiarized myself with the staff and equipment and then we waited for orders.

My bed and locker were in a large area where the Pictorial Center personnel lived. My roommate was a guy named

Jamile Farah. That was his real name. His professional name was **Jamie Farr.** He had just finished doing his first feature film, *Blackboard Jungle*. He played a mentally retarded student who kind of "saves the day" at the end of the film. The film starred **Glenn Ford**. One day, Jamie asked me if he could borrow my raincoat. I had a London Fog raincoat, along with my other "civvies." He told me he had been invited to a huge party being thrown by **Mike Todd** at Madison Square Garden, to kick off his new film, *Around the World in 80 Days*. I said, "Sure, you can use my raincoat. If **Liz Taylor** is at the party, be sure to brush up against her, so I can say my raincoat touched Liz Taylor!" Jamie was not assigned to Field Unit #1, so I only saw him when we were in town awaiting assignment. I'm sure you remember him as **Klinger** in the great TV series *M.A.S.H.*, which he starred in after his military service.

Our first assignment was to drive, in convoy, to Fort Belvoir, Virginia, the home of the U.S. Army Engineering School. We were to try to apply television to the training program. Again, I was pioneering another chapter in the early days of television. I welcomed the challenge! When we rolled into Fort Belvoir, we were greeted rather icily. But after we did our first "show," they couldn't do enough for us. Anything we wanted, we got.

We proved that troops could be trained faster and better with the use of television. The class on the "Assembly and Disassembly of the M-1 Rifle" was our first challenge. We built a studio with drapes as a background in a large, unused building. We had monitors set up in three huge buildings, where there were hundreds of soldiers sitting at tables with their rifles and an oilcloth that had the outlines of the different parts of the rifle silk-screened on it. In the classrooms, we had telephones wired to our control room. In the studio, we had an instructor standing behind a huge, oversized model of the M-1 rifle. The parts actually moved on the model. As the instructor removed a part, he would remove it over and over, while all of the students in the three classrooms tried the maneuver. I would cut to a close-up of him removing the part. When everyone in all three classrooms had completed the step, I was alerted by phone that they were ready for the next step. I would then cut back to the instructor, who went on with the next step, and so forth.

That first class proved that, with quality instructors, there was no limit to how many troops could be trained—all at the same time! We were at Fort Belvoir for a couple of months, and we applied television to everything from a small part on a Nike missile stand to a full-field maneuver. While we were doing the telecasts, we also made kinescope recordings of the classes for later use.

We returned to New York and waited for our next assignment. We worked a normal day and had our nights to ourselves. I usually dressed in civilian clothes and went into New York City every night. I saw as many Broadway shows as I could afford. But I spent a great deal of time at the apartment of my friend Danny Franks. We would usually sit around and talk and listen to records. Danny and his wife, Ruth, made me feel like a part of their family. They had a little girl named Susie, their first child. They now have six kids! Danny invited me to go with him one evening to visit a set he was lighting for an upcoming TV special. **Bill** and **Cora Baird** were doing their wonderful marionette work on the special. I got to meet and talk with them. Danny ran with a crowd of "up-and-coming" people in the business. He was close friends with **Carol Burnett,** although I never did get to meet her. I did spend a lot of time dining and going to movies with **Ken** and **Mitzie Welch**, who were comedy writers. And I spent time with **Romaine Johnston**, who was a set designer. All three of them, Ken, Mitzie, and Romaine, went to Hollywood with Carol and worked with her on *The Carol Burnett Show*. Danny didn't go with them, because he loved New York City and would not leave it. Danny later left ABC-TV and started his own lighting company. Through the years he worked on all kinds of fantastic assignments. He was the lighting director for all of the **"Billy Graham Crusade"** telecasts, all over the world. I still keep in touch with Ruth and Danny. But not often enough, really. I owe them a lot for all their kindness.

In the next few months at the Pictorial Center, we were sent on assignment to Fort Huachuca, Arizona, and we participated in a CBS-TV network special on Armed Forces Day, from Andrews Air Force Base in Maryland. One evening, I went down to the noncommissioned officer's bar at the Pictorial Center. The bartender was a sergeant who worked during the day in the personnel department. He said to me, "Ron, I just cut some orders today transferring you out of the Pictorial Center!" I said, "Oh my gosh, where am I being sent?" He said, "To Europe, I think." I was incredulous. I gulped a couple of drinks down, real fast. The sergeant continued, "Listen, you're a good guy. If you want me to, I can get you off of these orders." I said, "No, I am no better than anyone else. If that's where the army wants me, that's where I guess I have to go."

It's a good thing I didn't let the sergeant change my orders. The very next day, orders came down to send at least a dozen guys to Korea! Instead of Europe, where nobody was shooting at anybody, I would have been sent to Korea! That decision was the third smartest thing I ever did in my life.

Over the Bounding Main!

WHEN I BOARDED THE troop ship in New York harbor, on that cold and dreary November day, I knew that the trip to Germany would not be fun. There were 5,000 troops on a ship that looked like a sardine can in the Atlantic Ocean. The ship slipped quietly out of the harbor as I took a last look at the Statue of Liberty. I must admit, it brought tears to my eyes. The first two days on the Atlantic were okay. But it was cold and windy "topside." I volunteered for stairwell duty so that I wouldn't have to go up on deck while the ship was being "swabbed down." Stairwell duty simply meant sweeping down the stairs and landings on the ship. The morning of the second day, we all gathered by our duffel bags to get the daily "word" from our leaders. A young soldier was leaning in an open doorway, or bulkhead, as they say in the Navy. The bulkheads are heavy, watertight, metal doors. They are held open by a magnet. Suddenly, a couple of soldiers ran out through the bulkhead and tripped the magnet, allowing the bulkhead door to swing shut. In doing so, it grabbed the young soldier, who was leaning on the door, by the hand and cut one of his fingers clean off. Before any of us could react, two young soldiers sprang into action, as though they had rehearsed it a thousand times. One guy grabbed the wounded soldier's hand and raised it straight up in the air. He ran quickly with the soldier to sick bay. At the same instant, the other young soldier took out a matchbook, opened the bulkhead door, and scraped the tip of the severed finger onto the matchbook. He ran toward sick bay, finger in hand. I have never seen such quick action in a time of emergency. We heard later that the medics were able to sew the severed finger back on and save it. I'm sure those two young men who acted so quickly deserved medals. I'm also sure they didn't get them.

On the morning of the third day, we awoke to a terrible storm. The ship was rolling back and forth so hard that you had to hold on to something with every step you took or you would fall down. The storm continued, nonstop, for three days and nights. Hundreds of soldiers on board the ship got seasick. I was fine for the first two days of the storm. On the third morning, I awoke seasick, too. I tried to do my stairwell duty. But I finally couldn't take it any more. I lay down, spread-eagled, on a landing and stayed there, rocking back and forth with the ship. A sergeant came down the stairway and said, "Get up, soldier!" I lay there and said, "Go to hell, sergeant!". He saw my plight, laughed, and continued on his way.

We finally reached land on the fifth day, Thanksgiving Day, in Bremerhaven, Germany. The cooks had made a great Thanksgiving Day feast for the troops. Turkey and all of the fixings were prepared. I swear to you, not one soldier could eat their dinner! The entire Thanksgiving feast went to waste.

I went by train to my destination—Orleans, France. Orleans is a quaint little town located seventy miles south of Paris. My orders called for me, as a broadcast specialist, to work at the American Forces Network (AFN) radio station in Orleans. The trouble was that the radio station had not been built yet. So I was up for grabs! I was interviewed by the commanding officer and I told him of the screw-up. He could have sent me to the infantry. Instead, he assigned me to Special Services and I was given the job of managing the gym, located on post. I spent the next couple of months watching basketballs bounce on the gym floor. I got on the phone and called around, trying to get reassigned to an AFN station somewhere in Europe. While I was waiting for something to happen, I doodled out an invention on paper. My stepfather, who was a retired, self-made millionaire, was very interested in photography. Especially color slides. He wanted me to quit WXYZ-TV when I got out of the service and start a film production company in a building he owned in Detroit. My mother was also pressuring me to do my stepfather's bidding. Anyway, the invention I doodled out was a way to control two slide projectors with a silent impulse from a taped soundtrack. I called the invention the "Auto-Fade." I mailed my doodles to my stepfather, who had an electronics engineer make a prototype of the "Auto-Fade," and it worked! More about that later.

One evening, I was bar-hopping with some fellows in downtown Orleans. We were in a little café having drinks. The French were having big troubles with Algeria at the time I was in Orleans. Would you believe it? A half-dozen Algerians, armed with submachine guns and wearing ammunition belts around their chests, burst into the café. The café fell silent. You could hear a pin drop. The Algerians went up the stairway to check out the upstairs rooms in the café. I had hung my London Fog raincoat on a peg on that stairway. When the Algerians came back down the stairs, one of them had my raincoat (the same one that had gone to Mike Todd's big party) over his arm. They looked around and went out the door into the night. That's the last I ever saw of my London Fog raincoat!

I had bought a Simca automobile in Paris and could get around pretty well. I often drove to Paris for the weekend. I lived in a barrack located about five miles from the army base where I worked. In France, it doesn't snow much in the winter. But it rains a great deal and the rain freezes, about an inch thick, overnight. I would have to chip my way into the Simca, almost every morning before I could drive to work. The road to town was cobblestone, and the ice made it extra slippery. One morning, after chipping my way into my car, I was on my way to work. I came to a circle with several roads leading into it. I was only going about five miles an hour, when a man on a motorbike entered the circle. I tried to stop my car, but it slid. He saw me slide and panicked. The motorbike fell and he and the bike disappeared under my car. My car finally stopped and I jumped out, expecting the worst. The guy jumped up and began swearing at me in French. I had missed crushing him by an inch! I was so happy to see him unharmed that I wanted to kiss him. In France, if you kill someone in an accident, you support their family for life! Vive la France!

I finally got a transfer to AFN headquarters in Frankfurt, Germany. We lived in a castle on the Main River. The castle had a dungeon and even a moat. The AFN studios were located in a three-story building on the property.

Every year, all AFN announcers had to pass an audition conducted by the chief announcer of NBC Radio. That's how competitive AFN was. I passed the audition and was assigned to announce the news and do station breaks. All AFN radio stations broadcast at 250,000 watts. That is five times more powerful than the most powerful radio station in the United States. Our broadcasts were heard all over Europe and behind the Iron Curtain. Often, I would announce the sign-off newscast. By the time I got to my room in the castle and turned on my portable radio, I would hear myself doing the news. How could that be? I had signed the station off the air. What happened was, the Russians would "jam" our signal and continue broadcasting on our frequency. They had actually trained men to sound just like the AFN announcers. Myself included! The Russian announcer would continue the newscast and read the most outrageous propaganda stories you have ever heard. I don't think anyone was fooled by their "trickery."

A plastic-laminated card, identifying the holder as an "employee" of AFN and written in English, French, and German, was issued to each of us. We were treated like "superstars" wherever we went. We could go into almost any nightclub anywhere in Europe, show the card, and usually get our drinks on the house. Rhine-Main Air Force Base was located in Frankfurt. Many of the officers at Rhine Main were tied to desk jobs. In order to get their flight pay, they would check out an Air Force plane on weekends and fly somewhere. If you worked at AFN, you could wangle your way onto the plane with them and fly wherever they were going, for free! I flew to London, England and Lisbon, Portugal, that way.

I heard that the nighttime music show on our sister station in Munich was going to be open soon. The disc jockey was being "rotated" back to the states. The show, *The Munich Night Train*, was a two-hour show which ran Monday through Friday from 11 p.m. to 1 a.m. I politicked for and got the show!

Munich was a breath of fresh air compared to Frankfurt. "Frankfurters" are very Teutonic and gruff. "Bavarians," as the people of Munich are called, are friendly, cheerful, hardworking and love to have a good time. AFN Munich was located in the university area and housed in a mansion on Kalbachstrasse. There was a beautiful lobby and offices on the main floor. The second floor was a huge ballroom, complete with a grand piano. The third floor contained the studios. The next floor up was where we were billeted. In the basement of the mansion, we had a "cave-like" bar, complete with turntables and music. The bar was "jumping" every night and was usually packed with great looking women and influential locals. Our commanding officer was Captain Raymond Call. He didn't know anything about broadcasting. He let us do our own thing, most of the time. When he made a suggestion about our shows, we would politely say, "Yes sir, I'll do that." Then we would go right on doing what we had done before. Years later, I saw an article in *Time* magazine lauding now-Colonel Raymond Call as a hero in Vietnam.

I loved doing the *Munich Night Train* show. The theme music was the **Buddy Morrow** version of "Night Train," a driving, exciting recording. I got fan mail from all over Europe with requests to play songs on the show. Our music library was immense. Every wall, floor to ceiling, was packed with 16-inch discs, each containing a whole album on each side. We had on hand every kind of music known to man. I played a mixture of vocals and instrumentals on the show. I called my listeners "The Night People." And I told them to wear sunglasses at night, so that they could be recognized as "Night People." You'd be amazed at how many people took me up on that idea! When Hollywood stars or American recording artists were in town, they would usually stop by our studios to be interviewed on the air. I interviewed several stars, including **Rock Hudson**. I am ashamed that the one interview I really wanted to do, with **Helen Hayes**, never happened. I ran into Miss Hayes in a restaurant in Munich. I asked her to come to AFN and do an interview for the troops. She said, "I don't really like to do radio interviews, but since it is for our boys in uniform, I'll do it." I was to come to her suite at a hotel in downtown Munich the next morning around 11 a.m. to do the interview. The Oktoberfest, a week-long "drunk-in," was going on in Munich. If you've never experienced the Oktoberfest, you have really missed a good time. Well, the night before my interview with Miss Hayes, I went to the Oktoberfest with a group of friends. I got back to AFN very, very late that night. When I awoke, it was noon. I had stood up Helen Hayes! I was so embarrassed, I didn't even call her. It is something I am not proud of, but it happened. I hope she forgave me for being so rude, and I hope you will, too.

There are film studios in Munich that rival anything Hollywood has to offer. Big soundstages, back lots, just like Hollywood. On occasion, I would get a call to go to the studios and record voiceover English dialogue for foreign language films. They paid me well and it only took a few hours to do. It was difficult trying to match my English words with the lips of the actor on the screen as he spoke in a foreign language.

Sometimes the films were in German, French, or even Italian. I couldn't always match the lips on the screen. If you have watched foreign films on TV, you know what I mean. Sometimes it is quite funny to watch.

My roommate at AFN Munich was **Mal Sondock**. Mal was from Texas, but he only had a slight hint of an accent. Mal was the disc jockey host on the *Bouncing in Bavaria* afternoon music show. Mal was balding prematurely, a little overweight, and usually a little disheveled. We used to kid him about being so sloppy. But he had a great voice and did a great music show. Mal and I were friends, and he introduced me to some fun times and fun people in Munich. Somehow, Mal got himself a part in an American feature film that was being shot in Munich. The film was *Town without Pity,* starring **Kirk Douglas**. Mal played the part of one of the men who raped the girl in the picture. He did a good job with his role. Even today, when I see the film on TV, it brings back wonderful memories of Munich for me. Mal stayed in Germany when he finished his military duty. He learned to speak German fluently, without any accent. He became the leading disc jockey in Germany. And he recorded music as a singer. He also owned a recording and music publishing company. Not bad for a guy who couldn't keep his bootlaces tied!

Many interesting things happened to me while I was in Munich. One day, our program manager called me into his office and said, "Ron, Pan Am Airlines is having its first scheduled flight from Munich to Nuremberg to Berlin since World War II began. I want you to go on the flight and record the activities for our network newscasts." I got myself a portable tape recorder and headed for the airport. The Pan Am PR people went over what was to happen with me. There was a ribbon-cutting ceremony, with the mayor of Munich and other dignitaries present. I got the appropriate interviews. Then we boarded the plane and flew to Nuremberg, where that city's mayor and others greeted us. Another ribbon-cutting ceremony, with interviews, and we reboarded the plane and flew to Berlin. As we neared Berlin, you could see a distinct line from the air. One side, West Berlin, was beautiful. Tall, modern buildings and clean streets were visible. The other side, East Berlin, was in sheer shambles. It was a dramatic sight! I got a bright idea. I asked the stewardess if I could talk to the captain. She took me to the cockpit and introduced me to the captain and copilot. My idea was to tape record the landing into Berlin, from the captain's point of view. So as we descended into Berlin, I would put the mike in front of the captain when he talked to the tower. Then I would grab one earphone on the captain's head and put the mike near, so we could record the tower's response. In between, I gave a verbal picture of what Berlin looked like from the air. This continued until touchdown. We were greeted on the ground by the mayor of Berlin and other dignitaries. There was a final ribbon-cutting, some interviews, and that was it. It turned out to be a pretty good news story. Pan Am wined and dined us that evening in West Berlin, and we flew back to Munich the next morning.

My service time in Munich was a ball! In addition to my *Night Train* show, I covered parades, boxing matches, and all kinds of other events. I made a lot of friends with the "locals," and the nightlife was terrific! I took driving trips to Copenhagen, Denmark; Salzburg, Austria; Florence, Italy; and other cities and countries. As my duty time was nearing an end, I met an English girl named Diana, who was on "holiday" in Munich for several months. She was staying with a German woman who was a friend of her family. We started dating. Things got pretty serious. Then her "holiday" was over and she returned to her family, who was living in Glasgow, Scotland.

Every night, I would play the songs she and I liked on my radio show. She could hear my show in Glasgow. She wrote me often and I wrote back. About a week before I was to rotate back to the States, I made a decision. I was going to marry Diana! I called her and proposed. She accepted. Her family scurried around and somehow got all the arrangements made for the wedding. It was a fancy wedding, with all the bells and whistles. The night before the wedding, her father and brother took me out on the town for my "bachelor night." We went to a Scottish pub, where they pour scotch like you would draw a draft beer. No ice, no water, just straight scotch! Well, within an hour or two I became a crying drunk! Diana's father and brother took me home. Then they went back out to the pubs to continue the celebration by themselves. I thought I could drink with the best of them. Boy, was I wrong. The wedding went well. Diana and I drove off for a quick honeymoon in Loch Lomond. It was a beautiful, rugged area, but it was cold. After all, it was November. Diana and I returned to Glasgow and I flew back to Munich, where I prepared to fly back to the United States. Diana had a lot of paperwork to do before she could join me in the states. I had shipped my car back to the States ahead of my departure. When I got back to the U.S., I picked up my car at the depot in New York and drove back to Detroit. I was a civilian, and I was married!

"When you come to a fork in the road, take it!" Yogi Berra

WHEN I ANNOUNCED TO my family that I was married, all hell broke loose. My mother was mortified that she had missed my wedding. Luckily, Diana was not there to see and hear the explosion. However, she would pay for it in spades once she arrived in Detroit.

After the confusion died down, I went back to my job as a director at WXYZ- TV. It was great to be back in the saddle, calling shots. I was living with my family, temporarily. Every day, my mother and my stepfather urged me to leave the TV station and head up a new film production business they wanted to start. My stepfather, who was my mother's third husband, was much older than my mother. His name was Claude E. Cox. He had never been married before. He was a unique man, to say the least. In the early 1900s, he built one of the first internal-combustion engines. It is now on display at the Smithsonian Institute in Washington, D.C. In 1903, he started the Overland Automobile Company. One of his Overland "horseless carriages" is now on display in the museum at Greenfield Village in Dearborn, Michigan. He sold Overland to Willys, which later became known as Willys-Overland. Willys went on to build the Jeep. Later, Claude invented a flowmeter, which was used on huge test stands built to test automobile and aircraft engines. He got a patent on the flowmeter and started a business called Cox Instruments, where he also built test stands, utilizing his flowmeter. He licensed use of the flowmeter to companies all over the world. His was the best in the business. Due to the World War II demand, Cox Instruments flourished. Claude was truly a pioneer in the automobile industry. You can find him mentioned in many books on the early days of the car industry.

My mother and Claude hadn't been married long when she discovered that he had kept $600,000 in a checking account, with no interest, for two years! He was brilliant, but when it came to earthly matters, he was a strikeout artist.

Diana was able to enter the country and come to Detroit after several weeks of paperwork. We lived in a vacant house that Claude owned for a while. Then we got our own apartment. It was kind of rough on Diana. She had no family or friends here. My mother, while she was attentive to Diana, never forgave her for marrying me without her presence at the wedding. Things got a little more complicated when Diana announced she was pregnant.

I had been told by Dick Briggs at ABC-TV in New York that he would have a network stage manager's job for me in a couple of months. Upon hearing the news of our impending "family," I called Dick Briggs and told him that I wouldn't be taking the job at ABC-TV. I decided that I didn't want to raise a family in New York. Who knows what would have happened had I taken the job? I probably would have ended up in Hollywood, doing production. But as they say, "You can't look back." I also decided to leave WXYZ-TV and join my family in the new company they wanted to open.

The company was called Bartlett Film Services. We used the building where Cox Instruments had been located. We reworked it into a production facility. There were offices, a large soundstage, an audio recording studio, a presentation room, a darkroom where we could process our own black-and-white and color still pictures, and a film storage vault.

The real reason that Claude wanted to start Bartlett was to utilize the thousands of color slides and motion picture footage that were stored in our film vault. The slides and motion picture footage had been shot by Claude's friend **Andre de la Varr**. Andre had produced travel "short subjects" for **Warner Brothers Studios**. His films were shown in theaters all over the world. They would run before the feature film was shown. Andre was nominated eight times for an **Academy Award**, in the "short subjects" category. When Warner Brothers stopped producing short subjects, Andre went to work filming for the world-famous travel lecturer **Burton Holmes.** When Holmes died, Life magazine did a six-page story on his remarkable life. After Holmes death, Andre took over and traveled the country presenting live travel lectures.

We launched Bartlett Film Services with a series of boxed travel slides which we called **The Burton Holmes Travelettes**. We advertised the slide sets in *Holiday* magazine, *Travel* magazine, and a few others, on a direct-mail basis. The slide sets sold well and we were on our way.

The Auto-Fade was developed further into a working, portable unit. Since it was the only unit that could control two slide projectors and had the capacity to synchronize the slides to the soundtrack, we had a tool that got us into the doors of many advertising agencies and corporations. The Auto-Fade was used in all kinds of meetings and even to create "living" storyboards for TV commercials. We applied for a patent on the AutoFade, but were rejected due to the fact that none of the parts we used to make the AutoFade were unique. You have to create at least a couple of new things in order to get a patent on anything. I learned a great lesson with the Auto-Fade. We took it to Eastman Kodak in Rochester, New York. They loved it. Within a year, Eastman Kodak came out with a small unit that controlled two slide projectors. I won't say they stole our idea, but I'm sure seeing the Auto-Fade gave them the idea for their unit.

We also invented and built, on our premises, a transparency illuminator that could hold over 250 color slides. The unit had movable channels on pegs. By removing channels, you could also view 4"x 5" and 8"x 10" color transparencies. We sold the illuminator with ads in photographic trade magazines. And we hired a man to sell the units directly to industry. Our illuminator was very successful. It was bought and used by *Playboy* magazine, Lever Brothers, and many leading companies. Eastman Kodak bought over 50 of them for use in their photo lab. We took the illuminator to the Professional Photographers Show in New York. The illuminator was the "hit of the show." We sold enough units to pay for all the costs of our booth and our travel expenses. Macbeth Corporation, who was a major competitor, tried to buy the rights to the illuminator from us. I was so cocky over the reception we got at the show that I turned them down on their offer. Looking back, that was a big mistake! But as I said earlier, "Don't look back," so I won't.

Our work with the advertising agencies and corporations was very demanding. Every job we got had a "screaming dead-line." There were often jobs that required me to work 23 hours a day for as long as a week to complete. I actually slept on the couch in my office, and my wife would bring me a change of clothes every so often. The long hours were beginning to put a strain on our marriage. We now had two sons, 20 months apart, and they weren't seeing much of daddy! To add fuel to the fire, Claude, who really didn't participate in the business, had hired a bunch of people to do what he wanted to do. We had several people on the payroll, most of whom didn't con-tribute anything to the success of Bartlett Film Services. As a result, we weren't making a profit. I was working for "pea-nuts" as vice president and general manager. One of our ad agency clients had often said to me, "Anytime you decide to leave Bartlett, you can come to work for us!" When I saw that Claude would not listen to me about all of the "dead weight," I took the ad agency up on its offer!

It shocked my mother and Claude when I announced that I was leaving the company. But I had to do it. I was almost burnt-out. We had a lot of business, but we couldn't make any money. So I engineered a deal with the man who was our sales manager to buy out my family from the business. They actually made some money on the sale of the company, so I felt better about leaving.

What Goes Around, Comes Around!

WELL, HERE I WAS about to take a new direction in my career. Zimmer, Keller & Calvert Advertising (ZKC) was one of the most successful medium-sized ad agencies in the country. The client list included many "blue-chip" consumer accounts. But they had a good balance of industrial accounts, as well. I joined the agency as a radio-TV producer. Our department wrote scripts and produced radio and television commercials, industrial films, and sales meetings for our clients. It was a good place to work. I had worked with many of the ZKC people when I was doing work for them at Bartlett Films.

One of our clients, Vernor's Ginger Ale, sent me to Cleveland to produce a videotape commercial with a local talent named **Mike Douglas**. Mike's show was still only being seen in Cleveland. He had not gone national through syndication yet. The show went "national" in the late 1960s and was very big for many years. Mike was basically a singer. But he turned out to be a terrific TV host as well. Our distributor in Cleveland bottled Vernor's and a line of soft drinks called Cotton Club. The Cotton Club line has many flavors. I met with Mike before we began taping. He looked at the script I had brought with me and said,

"Ron, this script is okay. But I have an idea that would allow me to include all of the Cotton Club flavors and Vernor's as well." I said, "Okay Mike, we'll try your idea. But if I don't like it, you have to do the commercial the way we wrote it." Mike agreed. We used a "highboy," a unit on wheels that came up to about eye level, upon which we put a line of bottles. All of the Cotton Club flavors and Vernor's Ginger Ale were included. Mike spoke briefly with the small band that played on his show. Mike stood behind the "highboy" and cued us to roll videotape. The band started playing a Calypso beat, and Mike began to sing. He sang about each flavor of Cotton Club and also about Vernor's. He was making up the lyrics as he went. We grabbed close-ups of the products as he sang. It was fantastic! He got through all of the flavors exactly on time. I knew then that Mike Douglas was a name everyone in America would soon know. You know the rest of the story about Mike's career.

On another occasion, I did a commercial for Vernor's with **Bill Dana**, who played Jose Jimenez on the old *Tonight Show*. He did the spot as Jose, in a Spanish dialect, and it was hilarious! Vernor's was not sold nationally. It was only distributed in certain parts of the country. Vernor's is a spicy ginger ale. Not like the ginger ales that are normally used in mixed drinks. You either loved the taste of Vernor's or you hated it. **Sammy Davis Jr.** had tasted Vernor's on one of his trips to Detroit. After that, Sammy always kept a case of Vernor's in the trunk of his car. He drank Vernor's mixed with Bourbon. It sounds like an awful drink to me, but they tell me Sammy loved it.

Our biggest client at the agency was Stroh's Beer. They sponsored many sports events on television. One of my duties was to go to almost every Detroit Tiger baseball game. I would sit in the TV booth with **George Kell** and **Ernie Harwell.** George had been a great third-baseman for the Tigers. Ernie was one of the most renowned baseball play-by-play announcers in the business. Ernie and George are now in the Baseball Hall of Fame. George owns a Cadillac dealership in Arkansas. Ernie and I worked together years later, which I'll tell you about later. They were great guys to work with—very laid-back and unassuming. I would bring scripts with me to the game for them to read on the air. One Saturday, I walked into the broadcast booth and I saw John Wayne sitting and talking with George and Ernie. When Ernie and George saw me, they introduced me to **John Wayne**. He was dressed in an African safari outfit. Bush jacket, boots, and wide-brimmed hat—you know, the whole bit. He stood up to say hello and shake my hand. A great shadow fell over me, and I thought I was meeting a giant. He took my hand in his and my hand disappeared in his hand. He was a huge man with a big heart. I was exceptionally taken by his friendly, warm manner. I had met, "The Duke"!

Stroh's Beer also sponsored the Detroit Red Wings hockey games on television. My duties also called for me to go to the Wings games and produce the live TV spot, with **Bud Lynch**, who was the broadcast play-by-play announcer. Bud was Canadian and knew hockey well. He also only had one arm. Bud had served in the Canadian Army during World War II. He saw tons of action. In one battle, he was badly wounded. His left arm was hanging by a thread. A buddy of his also got hit, was badly wounded and couldn't walk. So Bud dragged his buddy several miles to a first-aid tent. In doing so, Bud lost so much blood that they had to amputate his wounded arm. I had the great honor of working with a true hero! Bud is now the public address announcer for all Detroit Red Wings home games at the Joe Louis Arena in Detroit. Bud is already in the Hockey Hall of Fame. He is loved and respected by all who know him. By the way, Bud is a wonderful golfer, too!

After a few months in the broadcast department, I got promoted to account executive. I was assigned to several accounts. In those days, the agency didn't have writers in the creative department. They only had art directors. So the account executives had to write all of the ad copy for their clients, as well as overseeing the accounts.

Two of the accounts I was assigned to were WXYZ-TV and WXYZ Radio. Small world, huh? I worked closely with the stations' ad managers. But I often had to meet with and present our ad ideas to the "top dogs" of both stations. In the case of WXYZ-TV, that meant I worked with John Pival, who was still vice president and general manager. A man named Chuck Fritz was vice president and general manager of WXYZ Radio. It was lovely to work on those accounts. It gave me a chance to see all of the people I had worked with when I was a director at WXYZ-TV.

I did a good job with both accounts, mainly because I understood broadcasting. I got along well with both general managers, too. One day, I had picked up some layouts we had done for WXYZ-TV. As I passed the office of our agency president, he called me into his office. He said, "What have you got there, Ron?" I said, "I have some layouts for the big 'spectacular' outdoor billboard we contracted for, on behalf of WXYZ-TV." I showed the layouts to my boss. He said, "These are the most exciting billboard layouts I have ever seen! When are you going to show them to the client?" I said, "Tomorrow." My boss said, "These are too good to wait for tomorrow. Let's show them to John Pival right now. I'll call him and see if he will see us today." What could I say? He was my boss. Incidentally, John Pival didn't really like my boss. He considered him a "brat" who had grown up with a "silver spoon in his mouth," as Pival put it. John agreed to see us if we could come out to the station quickly.

When we got to Pival's office, he called his ad manager to join us. His ad manager took one look at my boss and knew something big was about to happen. John Pival said, "Let's see what you've got, Ron." Now, you need to know that whenever we got an assignment from Pival, he would always have us do one idea "his way." He would pay for the work, but he wanted us to include his idea along with our ideas. So I showed him all of our layout ideas. Then, I showed him his layout idea. He said, "I like your ideas—they're good. But, I like my idea bet-ter!" My boss nearly fell off his chair. Pival's idea was dread-ful. My boss defended our layouts with every appeal he could make. But John said, "No, I want you to use my idea for the billboard." Then my boss, in a last-ditch effort, said, "I'll tell you what, John. You can call in any "bunny" in your offices. I'll bet you $100 that when she sees your idea and our ideas, she'll pick ours!" Pival said, "You're on!" But instead of calling in a secretary or some underling, Pival called in his general sales manager. This guy was so afraid of Pival that he literally trembled in his presence. John Pival said to the sales man-ager, "I want you to settle a little bet for me." I had spread the layouts out all over Pival's office, on chairs and couches. John then said, "Tell me, which layout do you think is the best?" He pointed to our layouts and said, "These?" Then he pointed to his version and said, "Or THAT ONE!" It was supremely obvi-ous that John wanted him to pick his idea. So he said, "John, I think I like that one best." John said, "Thank you" and excused his sales manager. My boss was ready to explode with anger. He slammed a $100 bill down on Pival's desk and we left his office. My boss didn't speak on the drive back to the office. He couldn't. He knew Pival did what he did just to put him down. That night, my boss called me at home and said, "Ron, I have resigned both the WXYZ-TV and WXYZ Radio accounts!" He continued, "But I have already picked up two new broadcast accounts, WJBK-TV and WJBK Radio. You will be assigned to those accounts, Ron." I was floored. It was a very rare thing for an advertising agency to fire their own accounts. Usually, it was the agency that was getting fired, not the client! The next day, I got a phone call from the VP and general manager of WXYZ Radio. He said, "What the hell happened? Why did you drop my account?" I said, "I'm truly sorry. You'd have to ask John Pival and my boss for the answer." I felt sorry for him. Little did I know that I would eventually go to work for him.

My years at ZKC Advertising were interesting and my work was varied. I was assigned as account executive on accounts ranging from sausages to dental equipment and broadcast stations. Probably my most important achievement was in securing and handling the Elias Brothers Big Boy Restaurants account.

There were three Elias brothers. Fred was the oldest, Louis was in the middle, and John was the youngest. They had gotten into the restaurant business by opening a diner called the Dixie Drive-In. It was a small restaurant with a counter and only pedestal seats, no tables. Everything on the menu was priced at five cents. Coffee, hamburgers, fries, dessert—everything was a nickel. The brothers borrowed the money to open the restaurant from their father, who had a successful donut shop. The brothers eventually opened a second Dixie Drive-In. All three brothers loved horses and horseracing. They ended up owning one of the most beautiful horse farms in the country, in Ocala, Florida. The brothers attended restaurant conventions to learn more about the industry. They had met a fellow named **Bob Wian** while at one of the conventions. Bob loved horses, too, so he and the brothers hit it off instantly.

Bob Wian is the man who invented the first double-deck hamburger. He had a small hamburger joint in Glendale, California. There was a group of musicians who came in late, almost every night, for a burger and coffee. One night, the musicians said to Bob, "Bob, we're tired of the same old thing every night. Why don't you serve something different?" Bob thought about it and got an idea. He took two hamburger buns and threw away the top of one of them. Then he built a burger with two patties, one-and-a-half buns, garnished with thousand island sauce and lettuce. He said, "Here guys, try this" The musicians did and they gave instant approval to this new kind of burger. They said, "What are you going to call this new sandwich, Bob?" Bob thought about it. He had a young customer who was a little overweight, wore coveralls, and had a pompadour haircut. He liked the lad. So he told the musicians, "I think I'll call my new burger the Big Lad!" He later changed the name to the **Big Boy**.

One night, the brothers were having dinner with Bob, who confided in them. "Fellas, I have a problem. The Frisch's restaurant chain has copied my Big Boy sandwich and my Big Boy character. They have renamed the burger the Big Lad, and they have a boy in an apron with a paper hat, running, as their logo. My lawyer says that unless I go interstate with the Big Boy, I can't stop them from doing what they are doing to me." Franchising was very new in America at the time. Bob Wian was a very unassuming person who didn't really realize the potential for his restaurant chain. He said to the brothers, "Listen, I like you guys. What would you say if I gave you the rights to open Big Boy restaurants in Detroit? I would only charge you an annual franchise fee of one dollar per year!" The brothers were immediately interested. But they had a firm and fast rule from which they never varied. All three brothers had to agree or nothing was done. So they said to Bob, "Let us sleep on it, Bob. Why don't we have breakfast in the morning and we'll give you our answer" The brothers stayed up all night long discussing Bob's offer. The next morning, they came down to breakfast and announced to Bob, "Bob, if you give us the state of Michigan for a dollar a year, we'll do it!" Bob Wian agreed to their offer. The Elias brothers were now franchisees, and Bob was operating an interstate business. He took Frisch's Restaurants to court, and they were forced to become Bob's second franchisee organization.

The Elias brothers had thirty-five locations when I began handling the advertising. At first, they operated their Big Boy restaurants as drive-in style restaurants, complete with carhops who brought your order out to your car. They eventually changed them to full-menu, sit-down restaurants.

Things went well on the account. Business was good, and the restaurant chain was growing. One day, I was in their office (all three brothers shared one office) making a presentation of some advertising copy and layouts we had prepared for their approval.

John Elias said to me, after they had approved everything, "Ron, you're doing a good job with our account. But you know, when you first started with us, you had two strikes against you!" I panicked. What could he mean, I thought? He continued, "First, you are young. This is a lot of responsibility for a young man. Second, you are Arabic. You know how we think (the brothers were of Syrian heritage and I was of Lebanese and Irish heritage), and we don't like people to know how we think." He then said, "But you have proven to us that we can trust you. So everything will be fine." I felt relieved and said, "Thank you, guys. I'll do my best to be worthy of your trust." And that was that. None of us knew then that one day, years later, I would go to work for them as a major player on their management staff.

During my time at ZKC Advertising, my wife and I, who now had two boys, divorced. She never got over the strain that Bartlett Films and my mother had put on our marriage. After six years of "trying to make it work," we realized we couldn't. I agreed to let her and our two sons live in the house. She had her own car. I paid her child support and took care of all of their medical expenses. I was living in an apartment and struggling to make ends meet. I brought my sons over to my apartment every weekend. My social life was relegated to Monday through Friday only. This arrangement went well for a couple of years. My wife, who was a very attractive woman, got into modeling. She began running with the "in crowd" of the modeling and photography business in Detroit. I began to worry about my boys after a couple of phone calls at night when they told me their Mom was not home yet and that they had not had dinner. The third time that happened, I went ballistic! I knew she wouldn't be at home when the boys were in school. So I left work early and waited for them to come home from school. They said, "What are you doing here, Dad?" I said, "Help me pack the car. We're going on a little trip." I packed the car to the rooftop with their clothes and toys and drove them to my apartment. That night, at about 9 p.m., the phone rang. My ex-wife was calling. She said, "Do you know where the boys are? Are they with you?" I said, "Don't you know where the boys are? You should, you know." She said, "Come on, I know they are with you." I said, "You're right, they are." She said, "When are you bringing them back?" I said, "Never!" Long story short, I didn't take them back to her. After much threatening and thrashing around, she finally admitted that it was too much for her to take care of herself and the boys. She also told me that she wanted to move to San Francisco, California. We sold the house and split the proceeds. I agreed to send the boys out to see her every Easter and Christmas and for several weeks in the summer. She went to California. The boys and I bought a house and took up "bachelor housekeeping" together.

In the Presence of Greatness!

FLASH BACKWARD IN TIME to a year or two after I left WXYZ-TV. A fellow director of mine at the station was very ambitious, and he had a vision. He wanted to produce a half-hour TV show for syndication. Syndication was relatively unknown at the time. Later, the industry would realize that a successful show in syndication could make more money than almost any network TV show could.

Somehow, my director friend had made contact with someone who would go down in history as one of the brightest, most intelligent, and most charismatic women in American history. Her husband had been one of the greatest Presidents in our country's history. Franklin Delano Roosevelt was his name. People call him FDR. His accomplishments are legendary. It goes without saying. They say that behind every great man is a great woman. It was never truer than in the case of **Eleanor Roosevelt**.

Mrs. Roosevelt had agreed to do a pilot show, with the hopes of syndication. My friend scraped together enough money to make the pilot show. It was an excellent show, with all the signs of becoming a strong syndicated TV series. Imagine the kind of guests a great woman like Mrs. Roosevelt could bring to the show. Half-hour discussions with Mrs. Roosevelt and an array of the most powerful people on the planet were sure to make for a classic TV series.

My friend needed financial backers for the show. A 13-show series was needed to be appealing to TV stations all across the country. It was decided that a cocktail party would be planned. The invitees would only be "movers and shakers" with the ability to invest meaningful money in the series. Somehow, my friend invited my wife and me to be guests at this small but powerful assembly. The party was "black tie" and was held in a suite at Detroit's finest hotel. I didn't have a tuxedo, so I wore my only dark suit.

The evening began with a screening of the Eleanor Roosevelt pilot show. It was powerful television. We all were excited at the thought of being a part of such a great television endeavor. Through the evening, the guests asked important questions of Mrs. Roosevelt. She spoke softly and deliberately. We all hung on her every word. Here was a woman of the world, with a great vision of how the world could be improved upon. Yet she was gracious, kind, and very warm in her responses to our questions. It was a truly spellbinding experience, and one that I'll never forget.

But when the dust settled, my friend was not able to raise the necessary funds to produce the remaining twelve shows of the series. Mrs. Roosevelt never did have a TV series, and the world was denied the opportunity to share in her immense wisdom.

When I look at television today and see the utter crap that is being foisted into our eyes and minds every day, I am sick at heart. I know that the Eleanor Roosevelt show would have ranked very high in terms of quality and content. It would have been a show we all could be proud of. Too little we learn, too late.

Broadcasting Beckons Me Back!

ON THE ELIAS BROTHERS Big Boy account, I hired **J.P. McCarthy** to voice the radio commercials. J.P., as everybody called him (Joseph Priestly McCarthy was his real name), was the top a.m. radio personality in the Detroit market for many years. J.P. had told me that he loved horseracing. I told the Elias brothers and they said, "Ask him if he would like to have a racehorse named after him." I asked J.P., and he went wild. J.P. McCarthy, the racehorse, was sired by **Needles**, who was a great Kentucky Derby winner. J.P. McCarthy won a lot of races for the brothers and Joseph Priestly. His close friends called J.P. "Joe." I'm proud to say I was allowed to call him Joe. He also did a live interview show around noon, from a trendy restaurant in midtown Detroit. One day, Joe invited me to join him for lunch and to "sit in" on the broadcast. His guest that day was **Mel Torme**, "The Velvet Fog." A lot of people don't know it, but Mel began his career as a drummer. His vocal talents are legendary. He had an unbelievable range and great control. His voice was like an instrument, smooth, mellow, and constant. The opportunity to sit and have lunch with Mel Torme was one I'll never forget.

Things were going very well on all of my accounts. At the time, I was handling the Big Boy account, the WJBK-TV and

WJBK Radio accounts, the Kowalski Sausage account, and one or two others. I had been promoted to senior account executive. But I wasn't happy with that. I thought I should be named a vice president of the agency due to the billing I was responsible for.

One day, the top account executive from WXYZ Radio asked to have a meeting with me in my office. He said, "I'm being promoted to local sales manager at the station. I think you would be the perfect guy to take over my list of accounts." I said, "I've never sold radio before. Do you think I could do it?" He said, "You're selling your clients everyday. Why not?" His list was the "blue-chip" list of the station. He had all of the big agency accounts. He caught me in just the right mood. I wasn't happy with the fact that I hadn't been named vice president, and I felt unappreciated. So I said, "Okay, let's give it a whirl!" When I told the president of ZKC Advertising I was leaving, he said, "Please stay! I'll make you a vice president if you stay." To me, it was too, late. I had made it a policy in my career to never ask for a promotion or a raise. If the management didn't recognize my contributions, I was soon long gone.

Well, the wheel of life had turned again. I was an account executive for WXYZ Radio. To think I was working for one of my old accounts. It wouldn't be the last time I worked for one of my old accounts. By the way, WXYZ Radio was the station that originated the great old radio dramas, like *The Lone Ranger*, *Challenge of the Yukon*, *Under Secret Orders* and *The Shadow*. The general manager of WXYZ Radio was the same guy whom we fired over the John Pival incident. We had a good laugh about it, shook hands and went on with it. I was at the station for almost a year, and I was fortunate enough to increase the billing on my client list by over one-third. I was pleased with my success in selling radio time, and so was my general manager.

I became friends with the morning personality on the station, **Dick Purtan.** He was a very clever and funny radio host. Almost every morning after his show, Dick would come down to my office, sit in a chair by my desk, and ask me for a cigarette. I would always give him one and we would sit and talk. I bought a pack of cigarettes that were new—they were made of grass. They were supposed to be safer, with less tar. But they smelled like burning grass when you lit them. Dick came down after his show, as usual, and bummed a cigarette from me. When he lit up the grass cigarette, he let out a howl, stood up and said, "What the hell did you give me? This is terrible." I laughed and said, "Dick, I'm only looking out for your health." Dick never asked me for a cigarette again. We are still friends to this day. He is on a different station now. But if I'm promoting a charity event that I'm involved in, he puts me on the air without question, which I think makes Dick Purtan one terrific guy.

Well, here we go again. I got a call one day from the station manager at WJBK-TV. His name is Jay Watson (actually, Earl J. Watson, but he prefers to be called Jay). I had really enjoyed working with Jay when I handled the account for ZKC Advertising. Jay Watson is the best "people person" I have ever known. He was brilliant, tough, and quick. But if he liked you, he had a heart of gold. Anyway, Jay asked me if I would leave WXYZ Radio and join his station as creative director/promotion manager. I knew television and loved it. So once again, I went to work for one of my old clients.

Before I relate my experiences at WJBK-TV, I want to let you read a poem that Jay Watson wrote on an airplane while he was traveling. It goes like this:

The clock of life is wound but once
and no one has the power

to tell just when it will stop
at late or early hour

Now is the only time we own
Live, love, toil with a will

Today, place faith with those you love
for tomorrow you may be still

Jay Watson

Those words let me look straight into the heart of Jay Watson. He is a wise man, and I have tried to live my life by those words ever since.

Working with Jay at WJBK-TV was a blast! We were a CBS-TV affiliate, owned by Storer Broadcasting. CBS was a power-house network in those days. They had Walter Cronkite, and most of their prime-time shows were number one in the ratings. Locally, we made our mark, so to speak, with local news. We had a great news team, and our newscasts were number one in the Detroit market. As Jay would say, "We're number one and getting one-ier!"

My job was to promote the station, both on-air and in the media, in order to attract viewers and create higher ratings. We wrote and produced our own on-air TV spots. And we wrote and produced thousands of print ads promoting our lineup of shows. We carried a few syndicated shows, which we also promoted.

I wrote and produced a commercial featuring two of the early greats: **Bob Barker**, host of *Truth or Consequences*, and **Mike Stokey**, host of *Stump the Stars*. *Stump the Stars* was the first game show to ever air on television, as far as I know. Bob Barker and I had something in common. We both loved miniature dachshunds. He had two and I had one. We talked for an hour about our dogs. Even today, Bob, as host of *The Price is Right*, asks people to get their dogs and cats neutered. He really loves animals and he really is a very nice man.

The Michigan State Fair is held every year in September. One year, our news anchorman, **Jac LeGoff**, was asked to emcee the evening stage show at the fair. The headliner was **Bob Hope**. The news director asked me to go along with Jac and make sure everything went well. When we arrived at the fairgrounds, Bob had not arrived yet. So we were escorted to his dressing trailer to await his arrival. Finally, he and his wife, **Delores Hope**, together with the nationally syndicated gossip columnist **Shirley Eder**, entered his trailer. Jac and I were introduced and we all chatted for a while. Then, it was show time. Shirley, Delores, and I were escorted to front-row seats at the side of the immense stage where Bob was to perform. It was a chilly September evening. Bob was already into his act and Delores, who was sitting next to me, whispered, "Ron, it's chilly. I'm afraid Bob will catch cold. Will you do me a favor?" I said, "Sure, Delores, what?" She said, "Will you take this shawl and put it over Bob's shoulders for me?" I said, "Delores, he is doing his act. If I go up on that stage now, I'll throw him off of his act." She said, "Oh, he won't mind. Please do it for me, will you?" I said, "Okay, but if he gets mad, you have to protect me." I decided to make a "bit" out of it. So I opened up her shawl wide, and in an exaggerated manner, tiptoed up the stairs and across the stage toward Bob. The audience saw this and a laugh ran through the crowd. Bob was surprised at the sudden laughter. It got louder as I neared him. As I approached Bob, I put the shawl over his shoulders and said, into the microphone, "Bob, your wife, Delores, thinks that an old man like you might catch cold in this cold Michigan weather. So she wants you to wear her shawl." Bob gave one of his patented pauses, looked out to the audience and back to me and said, "Tomorrow, we'll pick out the furniture, dear!" The audience went berserk; I turned a little pink and strode off the stage, back to my seat next to Delores. The applause was still strong when Delores said to me, "Don't worry, Ron, he loved the 'bit.'"

The CBS "Star Junkets"

ALL THREE MAJOR NETWORKS used to unveil their new shows, all at once, during the first week of September. Our network, CBS, would hold a "Star Junket," a two-day affair, usually in a hotel in Atlanta, Georgia. CBS would bring together the stars of all of their new and returning shows. The affiliate stations would send crews to film promotional spots with the stars. Every year, I would take a cameraman, an audio man, and an assistant to Atlanta and make promotional spots for use on the air during the fall announcement period.

CBS would "bicycle" the stars from one room to another. Each station had twenty minutes to film their promo with each star. We filmed promos with **Ed Asner, Cloris Leachman, Robert Conrad, Richard Dawson, Sandy Duncan, Mike Farrell, John Forsythe, Lola Falana, Ted Knight, Mary Tyler Moore, Jim Nabors, Loretta Swit, Jack Lord, Chad Everett**, and many, many more CBS stars.

On the last night of one of the Atlanta "junkets," my crew and I were at the traditional CBS "wrap party," to which all of the affiliates and the CBS stars were invited. I had brought Frank Judge and his wife Betty with me on this trip. Frank was the radio-TV critic for the *Detroit News*. I had set Frank and his wife up in a fancy suite in the hotel, complete with two bedrooms, a main room, and a wet bar. Towards the end of the evening, I found myself in conversation with **Eddie Albert**, who was starring on the show *Green Acres*, and **Ross Martin**, who was starring on the show *The Wild, Wild West*. We were having a good time, so I asked them if they would like to come up to Frank Judge's suite for a nightcap. They said, "Sure." I got hold of the two local talents we had brought to do interviews with the stars. I introduced Eddie and Ross to Frank Judge and his wife, and we all headed for Frank's suite.

We had a great time talking. Eddie liked martinis and Ross did, too. Frank's wife said she had a headache and excused herself to go to bed. Frank joined her. Eddie, Ross, the two local talents, and I continued the party. Ross, who was a very outgoing guy, was telling us about his role in the film *It's a Mad, Mad, Mad, Mad World*. In the film, he did a sword-fight scene with **Tony Curtis**. Ross was reenacting the scene, jumping on the couch and flailing an imaginary sword. It was an unbelievable moment. Suddenly, Frank Judge stormed into the main room and shouted, "You folks are disturbing my wife's sleep. Get out!" Can you imagine? Here were two big TV stars, giving of their time. Besides, WJBK-TV had paid for the suite and Frank and his wife's travel expenses. And he was throwing Eddie Albert, Ross Martin, and the rest of us out of his suite. I was mortified. I never did like newspaper people. Both Eddie and Ross realized the situation and were good sports about it. But in spite of that incident, years later, Eddie Albert agreed to film a promotional spot for the National Guard, an account I handled, for free.

J.P. McCarthy and I Cross Paths... Again!

JAY WATSON WAS A genius with programming. J.P. McCarthy, who was, in my mind, the best radio interviewer in the business, wanted to do television. So Jay created a show called, **"J.P. McCarthy, Sports on the Record, off the Record."** The show aired once every three months, as a "special." Every show was loaded with big-name sports personalities. On one show, J.P.'s guests included **Joe Frazier, Bill Freehan, Bill Russell**, and **Howard Cosell.** Cosell had brought along **Roone Arledge**, the head of ABC-TV sports. He later became head of ABC-TV news. My job was to take the "stars" of the show up to our conference room, where we had a wet bar. I would fix them a drink and sit and talk with them until just before airtime. Then I would escort them to the studio, where we had a live audience. I invited Roone Arledge to sit in the control room, since he was not appearing on the show. I noticed that Roone had brought his drink with him to the control room. Now, Storer Broadcasting, who owned the station, had a strict policy. No drinks were allowed in the control room... ever! So it became my job to get the drink out of Arledge's hand. I said to Roone, "I'm sorry, but you have to give me your drink." He said,

"You want a sip?" I said, "No, I want your drink. Drinking is not allowed in the control room." He gave me a look that said, "Do you know who you are talking to?" I took his drink from him and left the control room. I felt about two feet high and was very embarrassed. I really earned my money that night.

Oddly enough, while J.P. McCarthy was undeniably one of the best radio talents in America, with great charisma on the air, he had practically no charisma on television. As a result, he never did a lot of TV. He continued to be a top radio personality until his untimely death. He contracted a blood disorder. They searched the country in an effort to find a bone-marrow donor, but to no avail. J.P. McCarthy passed away quickly and way too soon for all of us who loved him.

The Donahue Decision!

ONE AFTERNOON, JAY WATSON called me to his office. He said, "Ron, I'm interested in a guy named, **Phil Donahue**. He has a talk show in Dayton, Ohio. I haven't met Phil or seen the show. So I want you to do something for me." I said, "Sure Jay, what is it?" He said, "I want you to fly to Dayton and view the show from the control room. I also want you to fly back the same day and write a critique of the show. You tell me what they have to do to improve the show. I also want your opinion on whether we should buy the show for our market." I said, "Jay, shouldn't our program manager be the one to do this job?" Jay said, "You have been a director. He wouldn't know what production changes should be made to improve the show. I want you to go, but don't tell anyone what you are doing." I said, "Okay, Jay," and I left his office.

The next morning, I flew to Dayton, Ohio. Jay had arranged for **Dick Mincer,** the executive producer of *The Phil Donahue Show*, to pick me up at the airport. Dick and I talked on the drive to the studio. The show had been on the air for three years. They did the show "live" with a studio audience. They were probably the first show that took calls from viewers while they were on the air. After three years, they only had a three-station network for the show. The show was only on in Dayton and two other markets.

We arrived at the television station and I was introduced to the show's producer, **Gail Love**, and other production staff. I also met Phil Donahue. He was a good-looking, tall man, with prematurely graying hair. Phil was a newsman with a flair for the interview. I liked him the moment I met him. The equipment at the station was old. It was, as we used to say, "held together with spit and bailing wire." I went to the control room with Dick Mincer and Gail Love and watched the show as it went on the air, live.

After the show, I had lunch with Phil, Dick, and Gail. Then Dick drove me to the airport and I flew back to Detroit. On the flight back, I wrote copious notes regarding what I thought about the show. I also listed the production changes that had to be made to the show. As an example, I recommended that they bring in a New York lighting director to light the set properly. Also, they had to add at least one or two cameras. There was a whole list of things that had to be done if the show was to look "first class," which it had to be if we were to buy it.

The next morning, I reported to Jay Watson. I went over the production notes and told him I thought Phil was great and that the show had a lot of promise. Jay called Dick Mincer and reviewed my production suggestions with him. Dick agreed to make all of the changes if we would buy the show. We did, and the promotional wheels went into high gear.

My staff and I started beating the drums with the press. We scheduled mini-shows in every major shopping mall in our viewing area. We had life-size cutouts of Phil Donahue, a live band, and we filled and handed out heart-shaped, helium-filled balloons that had "I Love Phil Donahue" silk-screened on them. We gave out thousands of them.

We did a lot of promotion on our air leading up to the premiere of the show. The big day came, and the "new and improved" *Phil Donahue Show* was on the air "live" in Detroit. We became the fourth station on the Donahue network. The ratings were good from the start. But Jay wanted great ratings. So we decided to do the show "live" for a whole week from Greenfield Village in Dearborn, Michigan. We set up in a church on the grounds of the village. It had seating for the audience. We loaded the week with topnotch talents. One day we had astronaut **Buzz Aldrin**. The next day, we had actor **John Gavin**, who was then president of the Screen Actors Guild of America. The next day we had the recording stars **Gladys Knight and the Pips**. On Thursday, we had the famous atheist **Madalyn Murray O'Hair**. On the final day, we were to have had the famous porn star **Linda Lovelace**. But the top brass of Greenfield Village refused to let us televise a porn star on their grounds. Imagine that; it was okay to have an Atheist on their grounds, but not a porn star! Go figure! So we scrambled around and decided to do the final show from our studios at WJBK -TV in Detroit.

We had put Linda Lovelace up at the Dearborn Inn, located near Greenfield Village. It was a long way from where our studios were located, and it was my job to get Linda to the studio for the show. So I picked her up at the hotel. She came down wearing a beautiful, full-length, shell leather coat. We talked on the drive to the station. She really was a friendly person, and smart. She told me some things about her and the porn business that are too hot for me to tell. So I won't. When we arrived at the station, I took Linda up to our conference room to await airtime. I said, "Linda, give me your coat. I'll hang it up. Phil and the others will come up here with you after the show for a drink." I turned around to take her coat. As she handed it to me, I saw that she had only a sheer scarf covering her chest area. No blouse. You could see everything! I said, "Linda, you can't go on the air like that or this place will be a parking lot tomorrow!" She laughed and said, "Okay, give me back my coat." She put it on and left just enough buttons open to be "legal." She went on the air that way and was a big hit with our audience.

The Greenfield Village week really put *The Phil Donahue Show* on the map. I got to spend some time with Phil and to really get to know him. One day, Phil invited me to have a drink with him and his sister, who lived in a Detroit suburb. It was nice to hear some of their family gossip.

Within a year or two, the Phil Donahue network had grown to fifty stations strong, thanks mainly to the show's success in Detroit. Phil had still been doing the show from Dayton, except for the Greenfield Village week. Now it was time to "move up to the East Side," so to speak. Phil made a deal and moved the show to Chicago. We still carried the show on our station. At that point, the Donahue network really began to grow. Phil's fame skyrocketed. And as you know, he finally moved the show to the "Big Apple," New York. He married **Marlo Thomas**, who was famous for her TV show *That Girl*. The fact that her father was **Danny Thomas** didn't hurt either. The sad part of the story is, after all the years of struggling to get to the top, Phil Donahue fired his loyal producers, Dick Mincer and Gail Love. I'm not sure why. I couldn't believe that he would reward their unwavering loyalty in this way. Shame on you, Phil!

Charlie Can Take Real Pride!

MY GRANDMOTHER WAS A "one-of-a-kind" person. She grew up in West Virginia, coal mining country. Most of the men in her family were miners. She only had a fourth grade education. But she was a truly amazing woman. She was a very successful drug salesperson for J. L. Hudson in the pharmacy. She dedicated her life to her family. A diminutive, unassuming person, she asked for little and gave a lot.

One day, she said to me, "Ronnie, I heard that **Charlie Pride** is appearing at the Michigan State Fair this year. Do you think you could take me to see him perform?" Now, I didn't know she even knew about Charlie Pride. I found out he was her favorite singer. My grandmother, who everyone called "Mom Webb," had done so much for me in my lifetime. She rarely asked me for a favor. I was determined to make good on her request.

A friend of mine was doing the lighting for the stage shows at the Michigan State Fair that year. I called him and asked him if he would save a couple of seats for the Charlie Pride performance. He said he would. So on the night of the performance, I took my grandmother to the fairgrounds. We made our way to the area where the show was to take place. My friend met us and asked, "How would you and your grandmother like to meet Charlie Pride?" I said, "That would be great!" We were escorted to the dressing trailer where Charlie would get ready for his show. Charlie wasn't there yet. He was watching the first game of a Detroit Tiger twi-night doubleheader. He would be along soon.

We waited, and I noticed my grandmother was visibly nervous. She never in her wildest dreams thought she would get a chance to meet Charlie Pride. Charlie arrived with an entourage. He introduced himself to my grandmother and me. I told him how much she admired his singing. He smiled broadly. Then he took her hand and kissed her on the forehead. He said, "Mom Webb, I am so happy to meet you. I'm very proud that you like my singing." He took out a glossy photo of himself and signed an autograph with the message, "To my favorite fan, Mom Webb. Love, Charlie Pride." He gave the photo to my grandmother and said, "I hope you enjoy the show, Mom Webb. It has been nice meeting you. But now, I have to get ready for my show."

My grandmother was speechless. She had never experienced anything like this in her entire lifetime. I'm sure that Charlie seemed bigger than life to her. And to get this attention from a famous artist was more than she could fathom. We were escorted to front-row seats and we awaited the show. The show began and Charlie Pride was great. He sang beautifully, and the audience was eating it up. Suddenly, Charlie said to the audience, "Ladies and gentlemen, I would like to introduce a very special person to you. She is my number-one fan, and I think she is my prettiest fan." The spotlight swung to my grandmother. Charlie continued, "Mom Webb, please stand up and take a bow. Let all of these fine people see how wonderful you are." My grandmother stood up. She was trembling like a leaf, and I was afraid she was going to have a stroke. There she was, in the spotlight. The audience erupted into thunderous applause. Charlie Pride had made Mom Webb...a star!

Mom Webb framed and hung Charlie's photo in her apartment. She put it where she could see it while she was sitting in her favorite chair. For the rest of her life, she loved to tell the story of how she had met Charlie Pride. Charlie Pride can take real pride in having made a little old lady very, very happy.

George B. Storer Had a Dream.
Or Was It a Nightmare?

STORER BROADCASTING OWNED WJBK-TV and several other TV and radio stations. Storer had also gotten in on the ground floor of cable television. The radio and TV stations were well operated and made big profits for Storer. The cable TV properties were experiencing a bottom-line profit of ninety percent. This was before the "city fathers" were educated to the fact that they could make expensive demands on the cable companies operating in their cities.

Let's just say that Storer Broadcasting and its employees were "sitting pretty." The profit sharing and retirement funds were bursting at the seams. Then, it happened.

The way I got the story was that one night, **George B. Storer**, who was chairman of the board of Storer Broadcasting, had a dream. The next morning, he bought **Northeast Airlines**. He did it on the strength of his dream alone. He knew nothing about operating an airline.

Everyone was shocked at this action. Why on earth would a broadcaster want to get involved with an airline? Believe me, it was a good question.

Northeast Airlines was a small airline that covered part of the eastern coast of the U.S. Its flights were primarily New

York to Washington, D.C. We all figured that George B. knew what he was doing. As promotion manager/creative director, I worked on the Storer annual reports. I noticed that the maintenance expenses for the Northeast Airlines fleet were enormous. It was in the millions of dollars a year! On top of that, Northeast had been struggling for survival for years.

As a result of this "dream" acquisition, Northeast Airlines sucked almost all of the profits out of the highly successful broadcast properties. The profit-sharing and retirement funds were raided to cover the expenses. This resulted in the employees taking the biggest hit. Their share of the pie dropped dramatically. Employees who had been counting on the profit-sharing and retirement funds for their retirement were in trouble.

The result of all of this folly was that Northeast Airlines was eventually merged into **Northwest Airlines**, who wanted the New York to Washington air routes. Storer Broadcasting lost millions of dollars and was never quite the same after that episode. One man's dream on one night had changed the destiny of so many people.

I guess you have to be careful what you ask for. You might just get it!

Big Boy Beckons Me Back!

THINGS HAD BEEN GOING well for me at WJBK-TV. I loved what I was doing and I liked the people I was working with. I married again. Barbara, my second wife, and I lived in the same apartment complex. She was a remedial teacher with tenure. Barbara was very good to me and to my sons. I was feeling a lot of pressure in trying to juggle my work and the raising of my sons. Marrying Barbara made my life a whole lot easier. We bought a house and the four of us became a family.

The program manager job at WJBK-TV was up for grabs. The current program manager had accepted a station manager job in another market. I was told that I had the inside track to be his replacement. The natural progression in broadcasting is that you go from program manager to station manager to, eventually, vice president and general manager. Not a bad career path to contemplate.

The only problem I had with becoming program manager was that the duties of the job had changed. In the early days of TV, the program manager was charged with the responsibility of dreaming up and creating new shows. It was really a creative job. However, with the advent of syndicated programming, there was little need to create new local shows. The job of program manager had been relegated to essentially overseeing the production personnel and doing the mountains of paperwork required for the station to "keep the license." Radio and TV stations in America were required to reapply for their operating licenses every three years. The FCC could pull an operating license solely on the strength of one viewer's complaint that a station was not serving its audience well. So every station had to present documented proof of performance to the FCC in order to have their operating license renewed. I didn't relish the prospect of doing all that paperwork.

About the same time, I received a call from Bill Morgan, who was executive vice president of Elias Brothers Big Boy Restaurants. My old client! He told me that John Elias, the youngest of the brothers, had developed a brain tumor and was dying. He had asked Bill to "go get Ron David to take over our advertising." John liked advertising, and he kind of oversaw it for the company. The other two brothers kept their attention focused on restaurant operations.

I was familiar with the company and I had a lot of ideas on how to improve their marketing and advertising efforts. So I had lunch with Bill Morgan. He said that I would have to meet with Fred and Louis Elias and some of the company's officers. I did something to protect myself. I wrote a job description and a list of duties for marketing director.

We met at Elias headquarters. Fred and Lou tried to tell me what it was that they wanted to hire me to do. Not being familiar with advertising lingo, they faltered. I pulled out my "job description" and handed copies to all in attendance. After I read aloud the description and what I planned to do for the company, the brothers said, "Yes, that's exactly what we want you to do for our company!" Fred Elias said, "You did that so well, you probably want to be a vice president as well as marking director, don't you?" I said, "No, Fred, I want to earn the title vice president. However, this is how much money I want to be paid as marketing director." I showed him a sheet with my salary demands on it. The brothers' eyes reeled. If they accepted my request, I would be one of the highest-paid employees in the company. They talked among themselves and finally said, "You drive a hard bargain, but okay, you're hired."

Jay Watson wasn't very happy about my decision, but he wished me well. He and I both knew that I would miss broadcasting. Well, here I was, going to work for the third time for a former client. Talk about "what goes around, comes around"!

Ronald McDonald Loses His Sense of Humor!

I DECIDED TO TAKE a month off before beginning my new job with Elias Brothers Big Boy Restaurants. But I had to cut my vacation short, because the brothers wanted me to attend a kickoff party to announce a new acquisition of theirs. They had acquired the rights to be the Michigan franchisee for the Roy Rogers roast beef restaurant chain. The press had been summoned, and **Roy Rogers** and his wife, **Dale Evans**, had agreed to make an appearance at the party. The Roy Rogers involvement wasn't highly successful. We only opened three locations in Detroit. The food was good, but the premise for the chain did not appeal to Midwesterners. After a couple of years, we dropped the franchise.

I spent a good deal of time focusing on point-of-sale advertising for the Big Boy restaurants. Most of our radio and TV commercials were small budget and centered on daily "specials" we were offering in the restaurants. I regularly hired a couple of guys that I had met when I was working at WXYZ-TV to produce the commercials. **Jim O'Dea** and **William Dear** had been working there as stagehands. Their fathers were stagehands, too. It is a tough union to get into. You almost have to be born into it. However, Jimmy and Bill were very ambitious. They both spent a lot of time and money learning to handle motion picture cameras. Jimmy went on to become one of the finest commercial shooters in the business. Bill Dear went on to become a film director. His most famous work was on the feature film *Harry and the Hendersons*. Bill also directed several half-hour TV shows for **Steven Spielberg**. For several of the "specials" commercials, we hired **Ed Herlihy**, who was the voice of Kraft Foods, to do our voice-overs.

I wasn't happy with the low-budget TV commercials we were producing. I felt that we needed better production values and better talent in our commercials. I also wanted to make most of our commercials' humor. Humor aids greatly in gaining viewer attention and in achieving memorability. I finally convinced the Elias brothers to let me shoot our commercials in Hollywood, where we could get top-notch talent and production facilities.

Our first Hollywood-produced commercial really got Big Boy a lot of attention. In fact, it also got us into a lawsuit with McDonald's Corporation. The commercial featured actor **Bob Sampson**, who had appeared in many feature films and made-for-TV films. The commercial was meant to be competitive with the fast-food chains. Bob talked about how limited the fast-food menus were compared to the Big Boy menu. At the end of the commercial, a clown comes into the restaurant and picks up a Big Boy menu. When he sees what is on the menu, he breaks into a wide grin and jumps up and clicks his heels. At that point, we "freeze frame" him as voiceover singers sing, "Have a choice for a change at Elias Brothers, have a choice for a change."

When we showed the commercial to our franchisees and company employees, they went wild with applause. When McDonald's saw the commercial they went wild, too, but not with applause. They sued Elias Brothers Big Boy Restaurants in federal court. They brought in a battalion of McDonald's lawyers. We had the good sense to hire a lawyer who was a specialist in trademark and copyrights. His name is **Bernie Cantor**, and he is brilliant. He reminded me of Henry Fonda when he addressed the court. We scoured the country and found hundreds of print ads and radio and TV commercials featuring clowns. Our contention was that our clown was not meant to represent Ronald McDonald. He was just a clown. Judge Joiner, who was presiding over the case, at one point said to the McDonald's lawyers, "Gentlemen, it is my opinion that if you continue to press this case, I could rule that your campaign line, 'You Deserve a Break Today' might not be copyrightable. You could lose it." The McDonald's attorneys were shocked. It took several months, but in the end we won the lawsuit. It cost the Elias Brothers several thousand dollars, but we got millions of dollars of publicity in the press and on radio and TV. It was a wonderful experience. We beat Goliath in federal court.

Rodney Dangerfield Finally Gets Respect!

ONE OF THE AD agency writers wrote a brilliant script featuring comedian **Rodney Dangerfield**. Rodney had been a successful stand-up comic for years. His career had diminished for a while. He spent several years selling paint. But he gave show business another try. When we met Rodney, he was on his way back up the "star" ladder. He was a great guy and very unassuming. In fact, he greatly disliked people who acted as though they were better than everyone else was.

We flew Rodney Dangerfield in from New York, where he had his comedy nightclub, **Dangerfield's**. We met with Rodney in a restaurant, on the evening before we were to film, to go over the script. The script called for him to say, after being served in a Big Boy restaurant, "Finally, I got respect!" The agency producer was very concerned about the line. He said, "I don't think Rodney will say the line. His whole career is built on not getting respect." I talked to Rodney about the line. He said, "Kid" (he called me kid), "do you think I should do the line?" I said, "Rodney, people will know it is just a commercial. It won't hurt your stand-up persona at all." Rodney said, "Okay then, I'll do it!" As we were leaving the restaurant to take Rodney to his hotel, in walked two superstars, **Diana Ross** and **Barry Gordy**. They saw Rodney and ran over to embrace him. Rodney introduced us to them. They obviously liked him very much. He has a way of putting people at ease.

We filmed another commercial with Rodney. It takes place in a fast-food restaurant. He is having a difficult time getting what he wants. He ends up in a Big Boy restaurant and gets the food and service he is looking for.

On the same day, we had to film another commercial featuring our seafood. The location for the commercial was in Malibu. We had rented the beach in front of a four-story house, which was owned by a young, wealthy man. As the client, I walked ahead of the crew, who were busily unpacking equipment for the shoot. I walked down a stairway to the beach. As I approached the beach, I saw a darkly tanned woman with long black hair and a black string bikini walking out of the water. She was stunningly beautiful. As she got closer, I saw that it was **Ali McGraw**! She said, "It's a beautiful afternoon, don't you think?" I said, "Yes, it is." She said, "The water is perfect for a swim. You should get in." I said, "I wish I could, but I'm working." She smiled, walked across the beach and went into the house next door to where we would be filming. I realized that the house she went into was **Steve McQueen's** house. By the time the crew came down to the beach, she was gone. But I'll never forget the beautiful vision I saw on that day.

I kept in touch with Rodney Dangerfield. We brought him into Detroit to entertain our franchisees at our annual meetings. He knocked them dead. A few months later, I called him at his apartment in New York. His Latino maid answered the phone. Rodney was sleeping. I had forgotten that the clubs in New York stay open until 4 a.m. I asked the maid to have Rodney call me when he got up. I left the house to do an errand. He called while I was out and my wife answered the phone. Rodney said, "How the hell are you? How's the weather there? May I talk to the kid?" My wife told him I had gone out, but that I would call back as soon as I returned. When I called him back, he was as friendly as he could be. I told him that I was on the board of directors for The Boys and Girls Club of Detroit. We were having an annual auction to raise funds. My idea was for him to allow us to have people bid on "winning a trip to New York and having dinner with Rodney Dangerfield." He said, "Kid, I love you, but I won't do it." I said, "Why not, Rodney?" He said, "Would you want to sit for a couple of hours and try to make conversation with total strangers?" I thought about it and I said, "I see your point, Rodney. Sorry I asked." He was right, and it further proved that Rodney was a no B.S. kind of guy.

Not long after that phone conversation, Rodney appeared on *The Tonight Show* with **Johnny Carson**. He made up a joke for me. He said to Carson, "You know, it takes about eight minutes to make a Big Boy. But it only takes a woman eight seconds to make a boy big!" Carson and the audience howled with laughter.

Rodney later got a new manager, who got him into feature films. He became very successful in Hollywood. He deserves it. He is a heck of a guy.

Hollywood Musings!

OUR REGULAR TRIPS TO Hollywood to produce television commercials provided some interesting situations. We once had a meeting with the great music composer **Sammy Cahn**. We met at his home, in his office. I have never seen so many **Oscars** and **Emmy Awards** in one room. He had shelves just lined with them. We wanted Sammy to write a jingle for Big Boy. He said, "I am flattered, but I don't write commercial jingles for any amount of money." We told him we understood his position, but we had to at least ask.

One evening, I was going out to dinner with our agency producer and a man named **Manfred Bernhard**. Manfred is the man who created the Big Boy character for Bob Wian. He also created the Big Boy comic book, which for over twenty-five years was a hit with the kids at every Big Boy restaurant. His father created the famous **Bernhard** typeface, which is still very popular today. Manfred was a very interesting man. He spoke with a soft German accent. He drove a Rolls Royce and had a three-story home just off of Sunset Boulevard, complete with his own tennis court. He had been married eight or nine times to different African-American women. His Big Boy comic book made him a very tidy living. Anyway, on the way to dinner, Manfred said, "I have to give a friend of mine a lift." We stopped at a small house in Beverly Hills and his friend got into the Rolls Royce. We all were surprised to see that his friend was movie great **Ann Southern**. She had been a top comedy star in motion pictures for years. However, she had not made a film in many years. She volunteered information about her financial problems. She actually broke into tears as she told us what a difficult time she was having with money. I thought it was pathetic and not fair that a star of her magnitude should be suffering so, considering the wonderful career she had. But Hollywood has a million similar stories to tell. Sad, isn't it?

We often used a voice-over announcer named **William Shallert**. Bill was the best in the business. He made a fortune doing voice-over announcing for the biggest advertisers in the country. You may remember him as the father on the *Patty Duke Show*. Bill also did and still does a lot of character roles on made-for-TV movies.

We did a pretty funny TV spot with **Tim Rooney**, one of **Mickey Rooney's** sons. He was young, good-looking, and very funny. He was great to work with. However, I don't remember ever seeing him in anything else after he did our commercial. I wonder how Hollywood overlooked such a talented young man. I guess it proves just how hard it is to make it in "Tinseltown."

We were filming in a soundstage at Raleigh Studios. During a break, a man walked up to me and asked what we were filming. I told him we were doing a Big Boy TV commercial. He looked familiar to me. When I asked him his name, he said, "My name is **Dick Wilson**, but you probably know me better as **Mr. Whipple** of Charmin tissue fame." You remember his famous line, "Don't squeeze the Charmin"? He wanted to chat. He told me that a while ago, the "suits" at the ad agency had dumped him. Charmin sales dropped off of the map. When they negotiated to rehire Dick, he really stuck it to them. He told me they were paying him over $250,000 a year for doing only a few commercials. Research had shown that people liked

Mr. Whipple, and as long as he was doing the Charmin commercials, sales were great. I thought to myself, "Good for you, Dick, or Mr. Whipple! It's great to see a good guy win!" The next time you squeeze a roll of Charmin, think of Dick Wilson.

We produced a commercial called "Mrs. Rich." The commercial called for a rich-looking older woman, along with her butler, maid, and chauffeur, to enter a fast-food restaurant and be disgusted with the menu and service. They leave in a huff. We discover them in a Big Boy restaurant, where Mrs. Rich and her crew are delighted with the food and service. It was a fun spot. Our "Mrs. Rich" was played by **Lucille Benson**, who had a major role in the movie *Silver Streak*, starring **Gene Wilder**. Her butler was played by **Ivan Thor**, who had a major recurring role in the television series *Room 222*. The good roles in Hollywood are few and far between. And in between, actors have to do whatever comes along if they are to eat regularly.

Things were going well with our Hollywood production trips. But at home I had some problems. My two sons were now teenagers. My second wife, Barbara, was having a difficult time coping with puberty and rock-and-roll music. Barbara was a remedial teacher, with tenure. She was very good at dealing with young children who had learning problems. But she could leave them behind when she left school every day. Living with teenagers on a 24/7 basis was more than she could handle. After six years of marriage, we decided the situation was untenable and we divorced. I, of course, kept my sons. We bought a house and set up "bachelor housekeeping" once again.

The Clio Award!

BOB SALIN AND HIS production company, Kaleidoscope, did numerous TV commercials for us. As I have mentioned, almost all of them relied on humor for memorability. We won Excellence awards at the **U.S. Television Commercial Festival** in New York City for a batch of our commercials. We were competing with TV commercials submitted from over 25 countries. "Helping Hand," "Trade-in," "Teddy Bear," and "Wedding" were the ones that won the awards for us.

My agency producer and I spent a lot of time with Bob Salin. As you might suspect, he took us to dinner often. One night while we were dining, a man walked over to our table and greeted Bob Salin like a long-lost brother. The man was **Albert Finney**, one of the finest actors to ever grace the silver screen. He starred in the movie *Tom Jones* in his younger years. His list of film credits is immense. Most recently, he starred on television as Winston Churchill. He and Bob had worked together in television, when Bob was an agency producer-director. He was very gracious to my agency producer and me. I thought to myself, "The great ones are almost always down-to-earth and unpretentious!"

Our greatest success was with a commercial called "Open the Hanger!" We cast two men, who had never done television, in the starring roles. **Dick Orkin** and **Bert Berdis** were well known for their hilarious radio commercials. They have written some of the funniest radio commercials ever. Dick Orkin is also the man who created the radio serial **"Chickenman" ...the most fantastic crime fighter the world has ever known!** The series played on radio stations all over the country. Every disc jockey in the country wanted to be a part of the "Chickenman" frenzy. The series was so popular that it was released to the public as a record album. Bert Berdis had been a radio writer-producer for a big ad agency in New York before he and Dick got together.

In "Open the Hanger," Dick played a wimpy-looking customer who is very impressed with the Big Boy menu. He says, "It's just like mama used to make!" The waitress serves him his meal and he asks to see the manager. Bert, who plays the manager, comes to the table and says, "May I help you?" Dick whispers in his ear and we cut away to some glamour shots of food with music and a voice-over announcer. When we come back to Dick and Bert, Bert is feeding Dick as he says, "Okay now, open the hanger and Mr. Potato will fly right in!" Music up as voice-over singers sing, "Have a choice for a change at Elias Brothers... have a choice for a change!"

The commercial was hilarious! But the most important thing was that it won us the coveted **Clio Award** for excellence in humor. The Clio Award is the highest award any commercial can win. It is the most prestigious award in advertising. And it is harder to win a Clio Award than it is to win an Academy Award. You compete against thousands of entries from around the world. If the judges don't feel that any of the submissions are good enough in a given category, they will not make an award. Only the best of the best win a Clio Award. You can understand my pride at such an achievement.

Dick and Bert had a stable of actors, some of whom were famous stars, doing the commercials they wrote and produced. We cast one of their people, a woman named **Miriam**

Flynn, in the award-winning "Wedding" commercial. Miriam also had not done any television before we cast her in our commercial. The interesting thing is that later, Dick, Bert and Miriam were seen as regulars on the *Tim Conway Show* on CBS-TV. After a few shows, they dropped Dick and Bert from the cast. But Miriam stuck. She later went on to have important comedy roles in many feature films and television series.

With such talent to choose from, it is no wonder we won awards and sold a lot of food to boot. I consider winning a Clio Award as my first "15 minutes of fame"!

Can We Talk, Joan Rivers?

JOAN RIVERS WAS ONE of America's funniest and hottest stand-up comedians. The ad agency wrote a couple of TV scripts that were meant for her to perform. When we asked her if she would do the commercials for us, she said yes.

Joan and her family had a big house in the Brentwood section of Los Angeles. A prestigious address it was. We made arrangements to go to her house on the night before we were to shoot the commercials. We wanted to go over the scripts with Joan and try to pick out her wardrobe for the shoot. When my agency producer, our director, Bob Salin, and I pulled up to her house, we saw that the grounds were protected by a high brick fence. There was metal gate and a box with a phone in it. We picked up the phone and a man answered. We told him we were here for the TV commercial meeting with Joan. We could see through the gate, and there were three or four huge Doberman pinschers running around the grounds. The front door opened and a man appeared. He clapped his hands three or four times and the Dobermans disappeared. The gate then swung open and we drove up to the entrance to the house.

Joan's husband, **Edgar**, greeted us and escorted us into the living room. He told us that Joan was just finishing up another meeting elsewhere in the house and that she would be with us shortly. He left us alone while we waited. The living room was huge and sumptuous. Everything reeked of money. Gold-plated lamps and dishes. There was a huge oriental rug covering the hardwood floor. Joan's daughter **Melissa** strolled through the living room and said hello to us as she passed through.

After a few minutes, Joan appeared and welcomed us. We showed her the scripts and asked her if she had any suggestions that might make the copy more custom to her style. She brought out some 3"x 5" cards and looked through them. They contained some of her stand-up one-liners. She made a couple of suggestions for changes and we said of course we would make the changes. Now the scripts were really suited for Joan and her type of humor. We had offered Rodney Dangerfield the same opportunity when we filmed with him.

We then adjourned to her bedroom to select the wardrobe she would wear in the commercials. She was very cooperative and made some good suggestions. We thanked her for her hospitality and then we left.

We expected the filming of the commercials to take the whole day. We rarely were able to shoot one commercial in a day, let alone two commercials. But things went very smoothly. Joan worked very hard and even made some additional copy suggestions as we were shooting. We were amazed to find that we finished both commercials long before the end of the shooting day. I thanked Joan for doing such a good job and for doing it so quickly. She said to me, "Ron, I just finished directing my feature film, *Rabbit Run*. I learned quickly that the crew could cost you thousands of dollars in extra costs if they didn't feel like cooperating with you. I had invested every cent I had and every cent my husband and even my father had into making that film. If the crew had wanted to, they could have really screwed me. As a result, I vowed that I would never give anyone a hard time or do anything to mess up a shoot from that time forward."

Happily, *Rabbit Run* was a huge success at the box office, and not only did Joan get her investment back, she made a lot of money with the film.

A year or so after we did the commercials with Joan, my wife and I were having dinner with some friends in the restaurant of a big hotel in Detroit. Joan was appearing in one of the show rooms in the hotel. She happened to walk into the restaurant while we were there. She recognized me and came over to our table. She told me how much she had enjoyed working with me and our crew. And she invited us to be her guests that night for her show. We gladly accepted. During the show, Joan acknowledged us to the audience, which I think was a very nice thing for her to do. The next time Joan Rivers says to me, "Can we talk?" I will say absolutely.

Joan doesn't do a lot of stand-up comedy anymore. Her husband Edgar has since passed away. But I see her on television, with her now grown-up daughter Melissa, doing interviews with the stars and making it fun and funny.

Coloring Outside the Lines!

DURING MY TENURE AS vice president of marketing for Elias Brothers Big Boy Restaurants, I was able to create some unusual projects. They helped set us apart from our competition. We were the first restaurant chain in America to offer a **Braille menu**. I worked with the Braille Institute in New York City to create the menu. We had noticed quite a few people with impaired vision struggling with our menu. It took quite a while to complete the Braille version of our menu, but the wait was worth it. Our vision-impaired customers were delighted with it. Many of them were drawn to tears with the fact that they could order what they wanted from our Braille menu without assistance.

The fact that so many Americans are overweight got me to thinking about how we could help them. Our menu was varied, but you couldn't say it was low-cal. In my mind, **Weight Watchers** was the best and easiest diet plan available. So I contacted **Florine Mark.** She is the Weight Watchers franchisee for the Michigan area. Florine is a dynamic woman. She has a great deal of charisma, energy, and drive. She also is the most successful franchisee for Weight Watchers in the entire country.

I told Florine of my idea, which was to create an authorized Weight Watchers menu to be served exclusively in Elias

Brothers Big Boy Restaurants. She loved the idea. She knew it would help all of her dieters to be able to eat out and still stay on the Weight Watchers plan. Florine set up an appointment for me at **Weight Watchers International**, which is located just outside of New York City. Fred Elias Jr. wanted to accompany me to the meeting. So he and I flew to New York and had our initial meeting with various top executives of Weight Watchers International.

The meeting went well. Fred and I presented our menu and the background of Elias Brothers Big Boy. We told them that we would like to work with their nutritionists to develop a complete menu that could be prepared and served in our restaurants. We also told them that we would do a lot of promotion of the Big Boy/Weight Watchers menu. In return, we wanted complete exclusivity in the restaurant business. They agreed, and we were on our way.

It took several months to develop a menu that we could prepare using the ingredients we had in our restaurants. Finally, the menu and recipes were completed. We set up a blitz press conference tour of the state of Michigan to announce the new menu. We covered every major TV station, radio station, and newspaper in Michigan in only four days. The menu was a great success and we received a lot of publicity for our new menu.

I mentioned, earlier that our Roy Rogers roast beef restaurants had been closed. We needed to do something with the three locations that had gone dark. Pita bread was just beginning to be discovered in America. Pita bread is actually Syrian bread. I am of Lebanese heritage, so I am familiar with it. Pita or pocket bread has been made since the Biblical times. It is very healthy, since it has very little sugar in it. Also, almost anything tastes great in it.

I began working with our staff nutritionists to develop a line of sandwiches to be served in pita bread. At the same time, I began development of a theme and name for the restaurants that would serve these new pita sandwiches. The name I came up with for the new restaurant chain was **Fast Freddie's Food Factory**! In addition to serving pita sandwiches, we planned to create a difference in the service at Fast Freddie's. What we served could be termed fast food. But our difference was that customers would be greeted at the door by a host or hostess. Once at their table, customers would be given a small menu, about the size of a golf scorecard, and a golf pencil. Customers were asked to check off what they wanted to order. Then a waitress came to the table, repeated the order out loud, and then went and picked up the food order and brought it to the customers' table. Fast Freddie's Food Factory was fast food with table service. No other restaurant in the country was offering what we were offering at Fast Freddie's.

We did a cosmetic job on the three locations. The inside and outside of each restaurant was made to look like a factory— exposed pipes and all! I worked with **Ted Petok**, who was a cartoon film animator. Ted won an **Academy Award** for his short subject, *The Crunch Bird*. Ted created the Fast Freddie character. He was a whirling dervish with arms and legs swirling. He had two big eyes and wore a railroad workers hat. He said, "Fast food and fun"! We dressed our service staff in railroad hats and aprons made of the same material as the hats.

We decided to introduce Fast Freddie's Food Factory with a television commercial that would incorporate animation of Fast Freddie over live restaurant action and food shots. We held an audition, or "cattle call" as it was sometimes referred to, in order to cast the commercial. Talent auditions are sometimes confusing. The talent agencies send over close to a hundred people in an effort to satisfy our casting needs. By the time you see and talk to all of these actors and actresses, you end up not remembering anyone you saw. We finally got our cast, though, and we filmed the commercial. We had custom music written for the spot. The commercial turned out great. Fast Freddie was leaping from table to table and the customers were enjoying the pita sandwiches and our staff of smiling people.

All three Fast Freddie's locations opened at the same time. Business boomed. People loved both the concept and the food. We were thrilled with our initial results. I felt certain that the Elias brothers were now on top of what could become a major new restaurant chain in America. The "fly in the ointment" was that they had assigned a very inept person to oversee the operation of Fast Freddie's. This person was successful in driving the new restaurant chain into the ground within a very short time. It nearly broke my heart to see the concept die. But my hands were tied. Today, everybody and his brother is serving pita sandwiches, but nobody has incorporated the table service concept into a fast-food restaurant.

But something wonderful came out of the Fast Freddie's Food Factory experience. I met the love of my life! I was invited to the grand opening of Gail and Rice Talent Agencies' new offices. When I arrived, they had several of their models, dressed in long evening gowns, helping guests to find their way around the offices. There was plenty of food, drink, and music.

As the evening progressed, I noticed that a stunningly beautiful model was looking at me from across the room. I diverted my eyes from hers and moved on. As I was leaving the party, I saw her again at the door. Three fat and balding advertising executives were hounding her to go out to a bar with them. I could see that she was very uncomfortable with the situation. So I butted into the conversation. I said, "Excuse me guys, but I have to talk to this lady." I then moved her away from them and said to her, "I couldn't help but notice earlier that you were looking at me from across the room. Do I know you?" She said, "You ought to know me. I auditioned for the Fast Freddie's TV commercial and you didn't hire me!" I said, "Well, you are too sophisticated to be cast as a fast-food waitress. That's why I didn't hire you. Why don't you let me buy you a drink as a way of making up for not hiring you?" This was her chance to get away from the ad guys, so she said, "Okay, let's go."

We went to a neighborhood bar near the talent offices. We sat at the bar and talked for several hours. I knew in a short time that I had just met the most wonderful woman I could ever have imagined. Her name was Cari. She was stunning, with the most beautiful eyes I have ever seen. More important, she was intelligent and warm. She had an unusual aura about her, almost haunting. I think I knew that night that we would be together for the rest of our lives. We dated a few times and I asked her if she and her six-year-old son, from her first marriage, would move in with my two sons and me. She agreed. After almost a year together, we looked and acted like a happy family of five. So Cari and I married. We are celebrating our twenty-fifth wedding anniversary this year. I have never been happier in my life, and I thank Fast Freddie's Food Factory for leading me to the one true love of my life.

Soupy Sales after shooting a Big Boy Christmas Gift Book TV commercial.

J.P. McCarthy and Stroh's Beer and WJBK-TV clients at a Detroit Adcraft (advertising club) luncheon.

Eleanor Roosevelt with TV series investors. That's me standing at the far end of the room.

Radio personalities, Dick Purtan and Tom Ryan with my wife Cari at the grand opening of a new Buddy's Pizza.

M.A.S.H. star, Loretta Switt with me and a couple of CBS-TV affiliate Promotion Managers at the Star Junket "wrap" party in Atlanta.

Filming on the back lot at MGM Studios. The Tarzan and Andy Hardy films were made here on the back lot.

Roy Rogers at the kickoff press party for Roy Rogers Roast Beef Restaurants. My first duty as the new Marketing Manager for Elias Brothers Big Boy Restaurants.

Sharing the Clio Award with Director, Bob Salin (left) and other Big Boy associates.

Rodney Dangerfield with me and Manfred Bernhardt at the Elias Brothers Franchise Meetings, held at the Main Event Restaurant facility in the Pontiac Silverdome.

Comedian, Joan Rivers with me and other Big Boy associates while filming TV commercials in Hollywood.

Phil Donahue with me and Producer, Gail Love, preparing to do a show at Greenfield Village in Dearborn, Michigan.

Phil Donahue and me at The Firemen's Field Day festivities at Tiger Stadium, where Phil addressed the crowd.

Newscaster, Lee Thornton takes direction from me on the set, as we film a WJBK-TV commercial.

Director / Cinematographer, Jim O'Dea, Assistant Director, Mike Rowles and me, as we film a Cadillac TV commercial, on location in Los Angeles.

Actress, Lucille Benson (Silver Streak), Ivan Thors (Room 222) with me and other cast members, as we film the TV commercial, "Mrs. Rich" for Big Boy Restaurants.

Soccer star, Trevor Francis, with me and SMZ Advertising employees, as we prepare for a soccer clinic at the Pontiac Silverdome, sponsored by Elias Brothers Big Boy.

Actors, Dick Orkin and Burt Burdis, with me and the agency producer, on the set of "Open the Hanger". The TV commercial that won us the Clio Award.

Actor, Richard Chamberlain, me and my wife Cari, discuss his outstanding performance as Henry Higgins in My Fair Lady, during a Cadillac afterglow party.

Detroit Tiger baseball Manager, Sparky Anderson, enjoying some pizza as we discuss the photo shoot we are doing at Tiger Stadium for Buddy's Pizza.

Golfer, Lee Trevino with me and the Central States Cadillac Dealers, during a cocktail reception for a Children's Charity Golf Tournament, sponsored by Cadillac.

Golfer, Arnold Palmer offers me "golf tips" at a Cadillac sponsored cocktail party.

Golfer, Larry Ziegler offers me still more "golf tips" at another Cadillac sponsored cocktail reception.

Basketball star Joe Dumars and me,
while recording a radio commercial for
my client, DTE Energy.

Circus star Gunther Gable Williams with me and crew members, during the
filming of an award-winning sales film for Hiram Walker Distilleries.

Find a Need and Fill It!

ONE MORNING, THE PHONE rang in my office. I picked it up and found Nick Kappaz at the other end of the line. Nick and his father, George, owned and operated the highest-volume restaurant in the Elias Brothers Big Boy chain. Nick told me that he had a problem that he thought I could help him with. His priest had been talking to him about the severe need for food for the needy in Southeastern Michigan. Thousands of men, women, and children were going to bed hungry every night. Nick's idea was to organize a canned goods collection drive to help alleviate the situation.

I became interested immediately. I knew that we operated 100 Elias Brothers Big Boy Restaurants in the Southeastern Michigan area. I also knew that we owned and operated a huge warehouse/commissary that had thousands of square feet of storage space.

I had been searching for some project that would truly make a positive difference to society. The light bulb went on in my head. I knew that this food drive project had the makings of something great. It could have immediate and lasting value for our community. Nick and I talked about how such a program should be administered. We came up with the guidelines, which are as follows: 1. We would only distribute the food to organizations that operated an ongoing twelve-month food program. 2. The food had to be distributed to people of every race, creed, and color. 3. The recipient organizations could have no state or federal funding. 4. The food would be collected from Thanksgiving through January 1st, but not be distributed to the poor until after January 1st. People are very generous and thoughtful during the holidays. But after the first of the year, people forget the dire need that continues throughout the year.

Believe it or not, the name of the food drive popped into my head as we were speaking. I said to Nick, "Nick, I think I have the perfect name for the food drive. We'll call it **Operation Can-Do!** Get it? Canned food, can-do?" Nick flipped out. He said, "Ron, that is the perfect name for it." So Operation Can-Do was born.

The Elias brothers gave me their blessings on the project and we went to work on it. I contacted my friend **Joe Weaver**, who was the top news anchorman at WJBK-TV in Detroit. He loved the idea and told me he felt sure he could talk his management into making his station the flagship station for Operation Can-Do. We knew we had to get the word out to the public, and WJBK-TV was the perfect way to get the job done.

We designed a logo that had the Operation Can-Do typeface crowded into the shape of a can. It was tight and very descriptive. We held meetings with our restaurant managers, our staff, and our truck drivers, who had the responsibility of picking up the canned goods from the containers at the restaurants and bringing them to the warehouse for weighing and sorting.

WJBK-TV produced public service announcements for Operation Can-Do and ran them on the air often. They did news stories on Operation Can-Do. Joe Weaver came to my house and did an interview with me for use on the evening news. WJBK-TV invited me to appear on a half-hour public service program they produced, to talk about Operation Can-

Do. The word got out to the public, big time, and our first Operation Can-Do food drive was underway.

We appointed a committee made up of dignitaries from the community to determine which organizations would receive the food and to determine how much food each organization would receive. That way, Elias Brothers couldn't get into any trouble with how the food was to be distributed.

The first year of Operation Can-Do went better than we expected. We collected and distributed three tons of canned goods. Each pound of food can serve two meals. So that meant that 12,000 meals were served to the needy in our first year of operation.

I am happy to report that Operation Can-Do has been conducted every year for the past twenty-five years. It is still going strong. WXYZ-TV has become the flagship station for the food drive. Last year, Operation Can-Do gathered 260 tons of canned goods for the needy. That equates to over 1,000,000 meals. Since its inception in 1978, Operation Can-Do has been responsible for serving 19,774,800 hot meals to needy families in Southeastern Michigan.

"Find a need and fill it." That's what Lord Kelvin once said. I believe that we did just that with Operation Can-Do. I also feel that this program allowed me to do something of lasting and meaningful value for my fellow man. I consider Operation Can-Do my second 15 minutes of fame!

And the Beat Goes On!

MY HORIZONS AND THE Elias Brothers Big Boy Restaurants horizons were about to expand. We were invited to bid on becoming the concessionaire for the new stadium that was going to be built in Pontiac, Michigan. It would be the home of the **Detroit Lions** professional football team. However, it would be used to put on all kinds of different events. Motocross races, rodeos, soccer games, basketball games, concerts, trade shows and many other events would be produced and presented under the dome of the new stadium.

Originally, the stadium was to be named the **Pontiac Metropolitan Stadium**. Along the way, the name changed to the **Pontiac Silverdome**. The Silverdome would become the second-largest domed stadium in the world. I think there is a domed stadium in Japan that is larger. The Silverdome seats 80,500 people. The sight lines are great for any event. **Barton Malow Construction, Inc.** built the stadium. It was completed ahead of schedule and on budget. No other modern stadium has ever come in on budget.

We won the bid. Now what? No one in the Elias organization had ever been involved with mass catering or souvenir and program sales. The Silverdome had many private suites and there was to be a fine restaurant on the premises. We scrambled. We visited every modern stadium in America. We observed how they ran their food, souvenir, program and catering operations. In Dallas, at Texas Stadium, we noticed that they used Boy Scouts to serve food in the concession stands and in the seats. The Boy Scouts were given a percentage of the sales in return for their services. We liked the idea and we determined that was how we would go for the Silverdome.

None of the stadiums we visited had what we thought were good facilities for the selling of souvenirs and programs. So I was given the responsibility of coming up with a better way to sell souvenirs and programs. I worked with a local designer to develop our souvenir and program stands. They turned out to be the best in the country.

I also was asked to come up with a name for the fine-dining restaurant that would be built into the Silverdome. The problem was that I was only given 24 hours to come up with the name. I stayed up all night writing potential names for the restaurant. The next day, I met with Fred and Lou Elias and other Big Boy executives to review my list of over 200 names. After much discussion, we all agreed on the name The Main Event. The idea was that no matter what the event, you should plan to dine at **The Main Event.** We designed a decor that reflected all of the potential events that could take place in the Silverdome. We commissioned an artist named **Mike Mikos** to create huge acrylic paintings, each depicting a different type of Silverdome event. The paintings were hung on the walls in the restaurant. I worked with our ad agency and we designed the menu. We used the actual covers of program books from every kind of event that might take place in the Silverdome as the covers for our menus. At a table for four, one person's menu might have a football cover, another person might have a soccer cover and so on. The menus later received a national award for design.

Every executive in the Elias Brothers organization worked hundreds of extra hours in preparing for the opening of the

Silverdome. A week before the stadium was to open, the Boy Scouts backed out of the deal. It seems that **Myra Wolfgang**, who was president of the Waiters and Waitresses Union, had gone to Boy Scout headquarters in Washington, D.C. She told the Boy Scout leaders that if the Boy Scouts served food and sold souvenirs and programs in the Silverdome, no union member in America would *ever* donate to the Boy Scouts of America again. Here we were, one week away from our first Lions game, and we had no one to serve food or sell our souvenirs or programs.

Bill Morgan, who was an Elias executive, had lined up the Boy Scouts to serve in the Silverdome. So he had to do something to make things right, and he had to do it fast! Bill contacted as many nonprofit organizations from the Metropolitan Detroit area as he could. He offered them the opportunity to have their organizations share in the responsibility of serving the food and selling the souvenirs and programs. Each organization would be paid a percentage of the sales for each event in which they participated. Bill pointed out to them that they could earn more money in a few hours than they could earn in a year of fund-raising events. Myra Wolfgang's intervention with the Boy Scouts turned out to be the best thing that could have happened. Not only did we not have to use union members as servers at the Silverdome, we were not locked into any single organization to get the job done. As a result, when people bought food, souvenirs, or programs during a Silverdome event, doctors, lawyers and top executives served them. They were all members of our volunteer organizations.

On the day the Pontiac Silverdome opened, the dome had not yet been put on the top of the stadium. It had rained the night before and we had to cover all of the food, souvenirs and programs with huge plastic tarps. The Silverdome storage areas were not meant to be waterproof. The yard lines had not yet been drawn on the football field. All night long, I watched as two helicopters hovered about fifteen feet above the playing field. They were using the wind from their propellers to dry the turf so that the chalk lines could be drawn. I was sitting on the floor in the Souvenir Room, wearing my hard hat, when I got a call from J.P. McCarthy. He was on the air. He interviewed me about the status of the Silverdome. He asked about traffic problems and what the public could expect when they arrived. I told his radio audience that everything was okay and to "come on down"!

The opening game was sold out. We sold over 25,000 programs before the *National Anthem* was even sung. Even without the dome being on, the fans were ecstatic with their new Pontiac Silverdome.

The event went off without a hitch. The next day, we had a meeting at our main office to review things. That night, as I was sitting with my family having dinner, I passed out and had to be rushed to the hospital. In the emergency room, they did a running electrocardiogram and even put nitroglycerin tablets under my tongue, thinking I might be having a heart attack. My entire life flashed before me. My wife was in tears. But the doctors finally determined that I was not having a heart attack. I was suffering from extreme physical and mental exhaustion. I am sure that many of the other Big Boy executives were as close to exhaustion as I was.

The dome was put on the Silverdome about six weeks after we did our first event. Life got a lot better for all of us and for all of the fans. During the first couple of years, the Silverdome hosted many, many exciting events. It drew the biggest names in the music world, due to its huge seating capacity. Artists like **Aerosmith**, **The Who**, **Elton John**, and **Elvis Presley** gave concerts in the Silverdome. As the concessionaire, we sold their souvenirs and programs and got a cut of the sales, which we shared with our civic group vendors.

When the advance people for Elvis Presley came to the Silverdome, I told them what percentage of the sales of souvenirs and programs we expected to receive. They balked at the figure I asked for. I told them, "If we don't reach agreement, you won't be allowed to sell anything to your audience. We have the exclusive rights to sell souvenirs and programs to the Silverdome audiences." Finally, I tired of talking. I said, "I want to talk to the Colonel!" The Colonel, of course, was **Colonel Tom Parker**, Elvis' manager. Colonel Parker arrived late on the night before the Presley concert. He was introduced to me and he said, "Ron, let's you and me take a walk and have a talk about the souvenir and program sales problem." He and I walked down to the floor of the Silverdome, where they had set up folding chairs. Colonel Parker said, "Ron, what seems to be the problem?" Colonel Parker was an old "carnival man." He seemed to care more about the souvenir and program sales than he did about the actual Presley concert. I said, "Well, Colonel, we have a lot of overhead as concessionaires for the Silverdome. We have to give the Stadium Authority a percentage of what we get. There are sales taxes, and we have to pay our civic groups 15 percent of what we earn." When I said civic groups, the Colonel said, "What do you mean, civic groups?" I explained to the Colonel that we used churches, schools, and nonprofit charity groups as our salespeople for the souvenirs and programs. The food sales, too. He lit up and said, "Ron, I think that is wonderful. I'll give you an extra 5 percent more than you asked for if you will pay your civic groups a little more." I said, "Colonel, we have a deal!" When the Presley concert ended, we had sold out every single souvenir and program we had to sell. People bought anything that had Elvis' name or likeness on it. Everybody was happy and the Colonel had renewed my faith in mankind. He proved that money isn't everything.

Life in the Fast Track!

WE HAD NO MORE than gotten the Silverdome operation up and running when we were asked to bid on handling the food, catering, souvenirs and programs for the **Michigan International Speedway**, located in the Irish Hills of Michigan. The MIS, as it is called, is actually a safer racing track than the Indianapolis 500 Speedway. The original owners of the MIS had run the operation into the ground. The new owner of the MIS was well known in the automobile industry. **Roger Penske** was a rising star in the racing world, too. He knew how to surround himself with top-notch people. He also was very good at using other people's money to get what he wanted.

We began negotiations with Penske and his people in March. The first race was not scheduled until May of that year. The concession facilities at the speedway were horrible. The race fans had been served their food out of shacks with dirt floors. We demanded that Penske build all new concession stands with cement floors. In return, we agreed to equip the stands with new cooking and serving equipment. I also agreed to do special promotions, tied into our Elias Brothers Big Boy advertising. The speedway called the time-trial days on Friday and Saturday "Picture Days." Fans were invited to bring their cameras and take pictures of the race drivers and their cars during the time trials. They usually only had a couple of hundred fans show up for the event. I promised Roger Penske that I would build the "Picture Days" event into a terrific profit-maker for the speedway.

During our negotiations, I was invited by the general manager of the speedway to have lunch with him and a rookie race driver named **Tom Sneva**. Tom was a member of the Penske race team. I found it interesting when Sneva told me that since the Indy car drivers were running at speeds of over 200 miles per hour, they only had a tenth of a second to make a decision if they got into trouble. If they made the wrong decision, it could mean death. I personally feel that race car drivers have a death wish anyway. Tom invited me to take a ride on the track in the speedway pace car. The car was a souped-up American Motors vehicle. It had to be able to stay ahead of the race cars as they rounded the track in anticipation of the start of the race. Tom had the pace car going over 120 miles per hour. Believe me, I was white-knuckling it all the way. Sneva stopped the car on the track, right in front of the grandstands, at the finish line. The track is so steep at that point that I couldn't believe the car didn't roll over. I enjoyed the ride that day, but I would never want to compete in a real race at those speeds. Tom Sneva went on to win the **Indianapolis 500** race a couple of years later.

We had a difficult time convincing Roger Penske to agree to the percentages we would earn on the food, catering, souvenirs and program sales. I had been given the responsibility of producing new souvenir and program stands for the speedway. Our food concession stands would be light years ahead of what speedway fans had experienced in the past. Roger was giving me a hard time regarding how I would promote the track in our Big Boy advertising. I told him, "Roger, the first race isn't until May. You don't expect me to promote the race in the middle of winter, do you? I promise you that you will be more than happy with how our promotion helps build your audience at the speedway." Roger finally calmed down and he signed the contract.

We had never been involved with a speedway before. Every Elias Brothers executive worked side by side with the workers we had hired to run the operation. Incidentally, we hired civic groups to serve the food and sell the souvenirs and programs, just like we had done with the Silverdome operation. Each group got a hefty percentage of what they sold.

The night before the first race, we had a terrible thunder and lightning storm. I remember carrying food and equipment up a steep flight of stairs which led to the private suites high above the grandstands. Lightning was flashing all around us. And here I was, along with the rest of the crew, carrying metal trays and equipment up those damn stairs. It was a miracle no one got electrocuted.

The rain passed, and the sun came out for our first race day. The fans were visibly pleased at what they experienced with the new concession, souvenir and program stands. They said out loud, "Man, is this the MIS, or am I dreaming?" I remember Roger Penske coming up to me after the first race ended. He had a smile on his face and he put out his hand and said, "Ron, I'm sorry I doubted you and your people. You all did a great job and I'm very pleased with everything!" He should have been. We tripled the usual sales of food, souvenirs and programs that day. The subsequent races that year were just as successful. We grew the "Picture Days" attendance to thousands of people. The stands were filled to capacity for every race. Eventually, ABC-TV televised many of the races from the MIS on national television. Roger Penske is a complex individual, but he runs a tight ship with whatever endeavor he undertakes. It is no wonder he has been so successful. Our involvement with Roger Penske and the MIS turned out to be successful, too.

To Thine Own Self Be True!

THE DAYS AND YEARS at Elias Brothers Big Boy Restaurants were busy, exciting and always varied. We had 200 Big Boy Restaurants to operate and market. Our involvement in the Pontiac Silverdome and the Michigan International Speedway kept all of us hopping. We were always creating special events to build sales. I put together a soccer clinic at the Pontiac Silverdome. **Trevor Francis**, the world-renowned soccer player who played for the Detroit pro soccer team, ran the clinic. We offered free tickets to customers of our Big Boy Restaurants. The soccer clinic drew over 5,000 young, amateur soccer players and their families. Of course, we sold them all the food they could eat while they attended the clinic.

A local television station invited me to a party to kick off their annual telecast of the **Jerry Lewis Labor Day MD Telethon**. Jerry Lewis was to be in attendance at the party. A close friend of mine had been hired by the Metro Detroit Chapter of Muscular Dystrophy to produce the Detroit telecast. She had worked for several years on the MD telecast. She devoted six months every year, day and night, to making the Detroit telethon a success. She was a tireless worker and was driven to make the Detroit telethon the best in the country. In fact, Detroit was successful in garnering the most donations of any city in America every year that my friend was involved the telethon. One of the account executives of the local TV station asked me if I would like to meet Jerry Lewis. I told him I would like to say hello to Jerry for my friend, who had worked so hard on behalf of the Jerry Lewis Telethon. I was introduced to Jerry Lewis and I told him I was a good friend of the woman who handled the Detroit segment of the Labor Day telethon. I told him her name was Mary Lou Zieve. He gave me a blank look, paused, and finally said, "Oh yeah, she's a helluva great gal!" I knew he didn't know who I was talking about. It made me sad to think how hard Mary Lou had worked, all those years, on his behalf. And he didn't even know who she was! I always donate to the telethon, but I have lost my respect for Jerry Lewis. He should know the names of the many local people who work so hard to make him successful in his work for muscular dystrophy.

One of the first things I did after joining Elias Brothers was to introduce video training into every Big Boy Restaurant. Every store was equipped with a video player and a color TV. Our training director wrote the scripts and I hired a production crew to shoot the training videos on location in the stores. We became the first restaurant chain in America to have "in-store" video training. I was in Toronto, Canada, editing the latest training video. We used the editing facilities of CFTO-TV. They had state-of- the-art equipment for video editing. It was also cheaper to work in Canada than in the United States.

My assistant and I had finished work for the day and we went to a coffee shop on Younge Street to relax. I noticed that **Artie Johnson**, one of the stars of the TV show *Laugh-In*, was sitting in the coffee shop with his wife. My assistant and I left the coffee shop to go back to our hotel. We were stopped by a red light at the intersection outside of the coffee shop. I looked up and standing next to us were Artie Johnson and his wife. While we waited for the light to change, I said to Artie, "I saw you on Broadway in *No Time for Sergeants*, with

Andy Griffith." I had seen the show in the mid-fifties in New York. Artie let out a shout and jumped up into my arms with his arms around my neck. He gave me a kiss on the cheek and said, "Finally, I have met someone who knows I am not an overnight success. I have paid my dues!" Inadvertently, I had made his day. Everyone thought that *Laugh-In* had made Artie an instant success. Actually, he had done a great deal of work in show business, years before the TV show came along.

The most surprising business deal I was ever involved in came by way of the **Detroit Tigers baseball club**. I had contracted, on behalf of Elias Brothers, for the advertising space below the clock in deep centerfield of **Tiger Stadium**. I had negotiated an addendum to the contract. It allowed us to build a huge metal version of the Elias Brothers logo and mount it above the clock. We also used the space below the clock for our advertising message. We kept it short. For instance, "Slide in on your way home!" It proved to be a good deal, because the logo extension above the clock could be seen from outside of Tiger Stadium. We therefore got millions of extra advertising impressions at no additional cost.

Everything went well for the first four years of our five-year contract for the sign. One day, a fellow employee came to me and said, "I just drove past Tiger Stadium, and it looks like our clock sign has been taken down." I called **Doc Fenkell**, who was the marketing and public affairs director for the Tigers. He had signed me up for the five-year advertising deal. I said, "Doc, what happened to our clock sign?" Doc said, "We are installing a new electronic scoreboard. It will be great when it is done. You can be on it for only $100,000 per year!" I said, "Wait a minute, Doc. We signed a five-year deal for the clock sign and only agreed to $36,000 for the whole five-year contract. We still have a year to go on the contract. What are you going to do about that?" Doc was silent. Then he said, "I guess you will have to take that up with our general manager, **Jim**

Campbell." I said, "Okay, make me an appointment, 'cause something has to be done about this situation."

Doc Fenkell arranged an appointment for me to meet with Jim Campbell to discuss the sign problem. Jim Campbell had a reputation for being a very hard-nosed negotiator. I was sure that I was in for a difficult time with him. I met with Campbell early in the morning in his office at Tiger Stadium. He got me coffee and was very cordial. Finally, he said, "Ron, what seems to be the problem?" I said, "Jim, simply put, your people have torn down our add-on sign and thrown it away. It cost us several thousand dollars to build that add-on sign. Also, we have one more year to go on our contract for the scoreboard clock position. Doc Fenkell wants us to pay $100,000 per year to be on the new electronic scoreboard. We only agreed to pay $36,000 to be on the scoreboard for five years. I don't think it is fair to do this to us." Jim Campbell sat back and thought for a minute. Then he said, "Ron, you are right. What has happened here was not good business. I think I owe it to you and your company to make things right." He picked up his desk phone and told the person on the other end of his line, "I want you to cut a check, made out to Elias Brothers Big Boy Restaurants, Inc., in the amount of $36,000." I nearly fell off of my chair! He said, "Ron, I am going to give you back all of the money you contracted for. Will that make things right?" I said, "Jim, you are probably the most honorable man I have ever done business with in my whole career. I thank you for what you are doing." A man came into his office with a check, which Jim gave me. We shook hands and I left his office. When I gave Lou Elias the check, he couldn't believe his eyes. It goes to show you shouldn't believe rumors you hear about people. Jim Campbell may have been a tough business negotiator, but he was also a "class act." If anyone ever tries to tell me something bad about Jim Campbell, I'll set him straight in a hurry.

Every year, we held our Annual Franchise Convention for the Big Boy Restaurants. We held these conventions in Miami,

Florida, for many years. We would hire top-notch entertainment for the banquet, which was held on the last night of the convention. We have hired **Henny Youngman**, **Rodney Dangerfield**, and many others to entertain our franchisees. The conventions lasted two days. We had meetings each day, from morning to afternoon, on various restaurant subjects. Most of the Elias Brothers executives were not good at public speaking. So in addition to my presentation on marketing and advertising, I was asked to do several other presentations at every convention.

We had moved the convention, one year, to Grand Rapids, Michigan. As usual, I was asked to make several presentations to the franchisees. My marketing and advertising presentation had gone well. The franchisees were delighted with our new ad campaign. I was making a presentation on "breakfast." McDonald's and many other fast-food restaurants had begun serving breakfast. And they were promoting the hell out of it. We had created a "mini-breakfast", which we could offer at the same low price as the fast food version of breakfast. Ours was a real breakfast with eggs, bacon, toast and coffee. Our breakfast was cooked to order and served on real plates, not plastic. So I told the franchisees not to worry, we could compete with the fast-food people. In my presentation, I mentioned the 5-percent franchise fee our franchisees paid us every month. I have forgotten why I mentioned the fee, but it was important to the point I was making. It was no secret that we charged our franchisees a 5-percent monthly fee. But for some reason, Fred and Lou Elias went ballistic at the mention of the franchise fee in my presentation.

At the cocktail party before the final banquet that night, I was standing with my wife, Cari, talking to some of the franchisees. The Elias brothers motioned me over to where they were standing. I went over to them, leaving my wife with the people we had been talking to. I could see that the brothers were angry. Lou started. He began poking his finger into my chest as he said, "Why the hell did you mention the franchise fee? I hate it when people mention the fee!" Fred also chimed in and was poking me in the chest with his finger. They were so loud that all of the people at the cocktail party could see and hear what was going on. My wife saw what was happening and she broke into tears and had to be helped to the ladies room. I, obviously, was very embarrassed with their behavior. But I bit my lip and said nothing until their tirade was over.

My wife was angry and so was I, but we went through the rest of the evening as though nothing had happened. When the banquet and entertainment was over, we went to our room. My wife said, "Why did the brothers treat you that way, Ron?" I told her, "I said something they didn't like in one of my presentations." She said, "That still is no reason to embarrass you in front of all of the franchisees and your fellow employees." I told my wife that the brothers were known for browbeating the relatives who worked for them. Why should I be treated any different? Like hell! I said to my wife, "Cari, if I let them get away with this, they will own me for life. I won't be able to look in the mirror at myself." She agreed. I said, "I am going to call Lou Elias in his room and give him a chance to apologize. If he doesn't apologize, Cari, I am going to quit." Cari said, "I want you to do what you think is right."

I picked up the phone in our room and dialed Lou Elias' room. He answered. I said, "Lou, this is Ron. I want you to know that if I said something in my presentation that you and your brother didn't like, that's fine. You have every right to chastise me for something I may have done wrong. The thing is, I think you should have taken me aside in another room to do the chastising. You embarrassed me and my wife in front of all of the franchisees." Lou said, "If you say something wrong again, I'll embarrass you again!" I saw red. I said, "Lou, you may get away with that behavior with your other employees and relatives. But you cannot treat me that way. Here's what you can do. If you don't apologize to me right now, you can take your job and shove it up your ass!" Lou was silent. So I said, "Okay Lou, I quit!" And I slammed the phone down.

The next morning, Cari and I had breakfast with some of the convention attendees and we left for home. We never said a word about the incident to anyone. On Monday, I didn't go to work. By noon, the phone began ringing off the hook. Every executive at Elias Brothers called me and begged me to forget what Lou and Fred had done and come back to work. I told them all, "When they apologize, I'll come back to work. Otherwise, it has been nice working with you!"

Lou or Fred Elias never called to apologize. And I never went back to work for Elias Brothers Big Boy Restaurants.

I was saddened that, after eight years of hard work and great success, it had come to this. But it had. I knew that if I let them get away with what they had done, I would not be the same man that I had been before. The Bible tells us, "To thine own self be true." I knew I had made the right decision.

Time to Fly on My Own!

I SPENT A COUPLE of days lounging around the house and contemplating what had happened with Elias Brothers. Then cold, hard reality set in. I didn't have a job. I had to make a living. So I thought through my options. I had done a lot of different things up to this point in my career. I had some talents. But which direction should I go in? I had been approached by several different fast-food chains to go to work for them. I didn't want to work in fast food. But I knew the food business. I had advertising agency experience. I had been a television director. Then it dawned on me. Why should I work for anyone else? Why not open my own business? And that's just what I did.

I discussed it with my wife and I called several business associates to see what they thought of my idea. They all agreed that I had something to offer. So I opened a business called **Marketing Viewpoint, Inc.** I would offer consultation services to businesses, and writing and film and video production services to anyone who needed them.

Marketing Viewpoint, Inc. took off like a rocket. I set up an office in my home with two incoming lines and hired a phone answering service. After the necessary stationery and cards were printed, I started making contacts. Florine Mark, whom I had worked with on the Weight Watchers menu for

Elias Brothers, put me in touch with the Pottiger family. They owned and operated **Entertainment, Inc.** They produced the huge books offering discount coupon for restaurants, movies, sports events, and hundreds of other entertainment venues. They produced custom books for every major city in America. The books were sold in drugstores and supermarkets. Charity groups sold them to raise funds. I was put on a hefty monthly retainer to work for the Pottigers and Entertainment, Inc.

Another friend of mine introduced me to the Jacobs family. They owned a small, but very successful pizza restaurant chain in Detroit called **Buddy's Pizzerias.** Their pizza was voted "Best Pizza in Detroit" by the *Detroit News.* The Jacobs family agreed to put me on a monthly retainer, too. I handled the marketing for the grand opening of their largest pizza restaurant, in Franklin, Michigan. I also handled print, radio, and TV advertising for them. We got Detroit Tigers manager **Sparky Anderson** to pose for a picture of him eating Buddy's pizza for use in a print ad. He was one of the greatest baseball managers of all time. Even better, he liked Buddy's pizza.

Dennis Silber, who owned the **Fred Silber Company,** put me on a monthly retainer to help him with his many projects. The Fred Silber Company was the largest supplier of carnival supplies in the country. They ran carnival midways in every nook and cranny of America, including the Michigan State Fair. The Michigan State Fair had been losing attendance. Dennis wanted me to create some new and exciting, "free" events for the fair. I was successful in convincing several companies to underwrite the cost of several new "free" attractions for the state fair. As a result, attendance grew rapidly.

Within a couple of months, I was making more money than I had with Elias Brothers. I did a lot of one-time projects for various companies. A producer at Simons Michelson Zieve Advertising hired me to be the producer on a sales film for their client **Hiram Walker Distilleries**. My fee was huge, and so was the budget for the film. The agency had contacted the Felds, who owned and operated the **Ringling Brothers Barnum and Bailey Circus.** For a fee, they agreed to let our film crew spend two weeks in New Haven, Connecticut, with the circus. A script was written, calling for all kinds of custom things to be done by the circus performers and animals for our filming. We went to New Haven and began our filming. The "Greatest Show on Earth" is really just that. The circus people are the greatest people in the world, too. They bent over backwards to facilitate our filming needs.

Gunther Gable Williams, the great lion, tiger, and leopard trainer, did some spectacular things with the wild cats for our film. For example, we set up a display of Two Fingers Tequila and Gunther walked toward the camera with a leopard draped over his shoulders. The leopard did not like the hot lights we had trained on the set. He balked many times. But finally, we got a good take. Gunther also trained elephants to hold huge silk banners in their trunks and rise up on their hind legs to show the banners, which had the logos of various Hiram Walker products on them, to the camera. We filmed several live performances of the circus. Late one night, the "comedy clowns" did a custom act in their bar room set just for our film. We loved working with all of the circus performers. They are very special people. The film was a great success. It sold a lot of Hiram Walker products to their distributors. And the film won us a Bronze Award from the International Film and TV Festival of New York.

I came home from New Haven. I had showered that morning and I had on clean clothes. But when I walked into our kitchen, my wife said, "Oh my gosh, you smell like elephant dung! Get out into the garage and take off all of your clothes, right now!" I had spent so much time with the sights and smells of the circus that it was oozing out of my pores.

I contracted with WJBK-TV to write, produce, and direct a series of television commercials to introduce their new anchorperson, **Lee Thornton**, to the Detroit market. Lee had been a political reporter in Washington, D.C. and came to the station with great credentials. It was important to make her a success in Detroit television.

The first year of operation of Marketing Viewpoint flew by in a flash. I felt confident that my new business would continue to be successful. Then I got a phone call that would change everything, again.

It Glittered...
but It Sure Wasn't Gold!

THINGS CHANGED WHEN I got a phone call from Mort Zieve, who was chairman of the Board of Simons Michelson Zieve Advertising (SMZ). Mort and I had worked together at WXYZ-TV. I had hired SMZ Advertising to do the advertising for Bartlett Film Services. Later, when I joined Elias Brothers, I fired Ross Roy Advertising and gave the Elias Brothers Big Boy Restaurants account to Mort and SMZ Advertising. I knew Mort's partner, Jim Michelson, too. They were both hardworking, trustworthy people.

Mort asked me to come to his office to discuss what he termed "a chance-of-a-lifetime opportunity" for me. When I arrived at his office, Mort and his partner, Jim, explained to me that they were forming a new corporation and that they wanted me to be its president. They went on to explain. One of their clients was **American Speedy Printing Centers**. **Vern Buchanan** was president of American Speedy Printing Centers. Vern was to be a partner in the new corporation, along with Mort, Jim, and me. The final partner was **Jeff Miro**, who was an attorney. His biggest client was mega-businessman **Al Taubman**. Jeff had helped Taubman complete the biggest land deal in the history of America. It had to do with the purchase of a huge hunk of property in Irvine, California. The deal was worth billions of dollars.

The four of us, Mort, Jim, Jeff, and I, were to purchase the rights to open and operate ten American Speedy Printing Centers. We would all be equal partners in the deal. As president, I would run the entire operation and they would not be involved on a day-today basis. Vern Buchanan felt that our best opportunity would be to open our printing centers in Jacksonville, Florida. Jacksonville is the second largest city in the world, in terms of square miles. It was a banking, insurance and military center. Vern told us that Jacksonville was the best-kept secret in America and that it would soon boom.

I hadn't envisioned such a drastic step. But my partners assured me that within a couple of years we would all be "rolling in dough." With Vern, who owned American Speedy Printing Centers, Jeff, who was a respected attorney, and Mort and Jim, whom I knew and trusted, as partners, I felt comfortable about joining them in this venture.

Vern Buchanan was pushing very hard to get the venture going quickly. So I closed my company, Marketing Viewpoint, and turned my full attention to the new corporation, which was called 1082 Corporation. It was named to help us remember when it was formed, October1982 (10/82). I was provided with a new company car. I drove to Jacksonville to scout a location for our first American Speedy Printing Center.

I found a real estate man who seemed sharp and we found a location that was near a freeway and in a fairly high-density population area. The real estate man also helped me find a house I could rent for my family and me. That being done, I drove back home. We put our house up for sale and my family and I drove back to Jacksonville, Florida, our new home.

My wife Cari and I were excited about the prospect of living in a warm climate. We also felt that we were on top of something good. I was able to get the first printing center up and running within thirty days. Believe me, that is very fast. Cari and I had gone through an intensive one-week training course on printing at American Speedy Headquarters before we left for Florida. We were a little shaky about our skills, but we felt we knew enough to get started.

Cari loved the house I had rented. Our neighbors were the Karams. **Bernie Karam** was with the **Secret Service**. He and his family came out to greet us as our furniture was being unloaded into our new house. Bernie said, "You are Ron and Cari David. Your cousin, Joel Webb, is also with the Secret Service." Can you believe it? He knew our names and a whole lot more, without ever having met us. Our government knows a lot more about all of us than we think they know. Bernie astounded me again a few months later, when a man passed a bad check to me for some printing I had done for him. I told Bernie what had happened one night when we were at his house playing gin rummy. The next morning, Bernie came to our printing center and pulled out a file on the man who had passed me the bad check. The file was complete with his name, address and even photos of him. I took the file to the man's house and told him that the Secret Service would come down on him if he didn't give me the money he owed me. I got my money, right then and there. Believe me, it is good to have a friend in the Secret Service. I couldn't believe how fast Bernie had tracked the guy down.

The Karams' made Jacksonville livable for Cari and me. They were good neighbors and good friends. But I soon found out what the term "good 'ol boy" meant in the South. I knew the advertising agencies' lingo. So I called on every ad agency in Jacksonville in an attempt to get printing jobs. I also called on insurance companies and hospitals. Cari worked part-time in the printing center so that I could go out each day and call on as many Jacksonville businesses as possible. We got enough work to get our printing center up and running. The people I called on were very nice to me. But all too often, I found that when my back was turned, they would give their business to the "good 'ol boy" down the block, who was from the South. I lost two huge printing jobs because the person I quoted to went down the block and gave the job to another local printer. They told the printer what I had quoted and gave them the job for a dollar less than I had quoted. It happened to me too many times. I was furious.

I worked feverishly to get the business going. We had hired a staff printer so that I could spend more time out selling. Cari managed the center in my absence. Our son, Derek, who was an "all-A" student while in Detroit, complained that the school was giving him work that he had done two years earlier. I had enrolled him into the best private school in Jacksonville. And this was the kind of education they were offering. Derek began to tune out of school. His grades dropped. I had been working so hard that I lost two pant sizes.

One night, after almost a year in Jacksonville, I came home for dinner. After we finished our meal, Cari said, "Ron, Derek and I have come to a decision. We are both very unhappy, here in Jacksonville. We have decided that we are going home to Michigan. Are you coming with us?" I was shocked to hear what she had said. But I thought about it. She and Derek were right. The business was not going nearly as well as we had hoped, in spite of all the effort we had expended. Derek was not doing well in school. And Cari was not happy with the whole situation. I knew they meant it when they said they were going to leave. I couldn't let that happen. I called my partners in Detroit and told them that I wanted out of the corporation and that they needed to find someone to take my place. I asked for my initial investment to be returned to me. To my surprise, they agreed to give me back the money I had invested in the corporation.

Cari suggested that I call a friend of mine in Detroit and ask him for a job. Mike Marontate had been an account executive at SMZ Advertising when I was their client. He later left SMZ and opened his own advertising agency. Over the years, Mike had asked me to go to work for him many times. When I called Mike, he said, sure, fly up to Detroit so we can discuss the details. Mike and I had a good meeting and I was hired as vice president and account supervisor of his ad agency, Marontate & Company.

My partners in 1082 Corporation were not happy with my leaving. But if I have to choose between business and my loved ones, the business loses. I was just as relieved as my family to be out from under the printing business. The prospect of returning to advertising, a business that I knew a lot more about than printing, was very exciting.

Luckily, our house in Detroit had not sold. The house market had been lousy and we had not received any decent offers for the house. So we packed up and drove back to Detroit. I had a feeling something good was about to happen. And it did.

You Can Come Home!

WE WERE THRILLED TO be back home. I had to turn in my company car. And we had to pay our own moving expenses back to Detroit. But it was a small price to pay. Our son, Derek, was back to school in Troy, Michigan, and his grades improved immediately. Cari was happy to be home and with her friends and neighbors. And I was looking forward to the future with great anticipation.

Marontate & Company Advertising had offices on the 9th floor of the Renaissance Center, Tower 400, in downtown Detroit. It was a small agency with only a handful of employees. The major accounts were several Hollywood film production companies. Marontate placed all of the print, radio, and TV ads for **Warner Brothers**, **Miramax**, **Tri-Star**, and a few others. Mike Marontate had made a deal with Milt London, who had controlled about 70 percent of all the movie business in Detroit for many years. Mike had some kind of financial arrangement with London whereby Marontate & Company did the work, but they both profited from the movie business accounts. The bulk of the advertising for the movies was placed in print. Mike's staff would resize the ads that Hollywood provided, buy the newspaper space and place the print ads in the papers. It was a very lucrative arrangement.

Movie ads run seven days a week, 365 days a year. Mike was on top of a real "cash cow" with the movie business.

Marontate & Company also had a few other accounts. The **AAMCO Transmissions** account was his major account other than the movie business. Mike had welcomed me aboard in hopes that I could bring in new accounts to help put more balance between the movie business and his other accounts. I was given a new car and an office with a great view of Hart Plaza, the Detroit River, the Ambassador Bridge to Canada and Windsor, Canada. Within a few weeks, we had a great opportunity to add new accounts to the agency. **Burton Advertising, Inc.** had been a respected advertising agency in Detroit for many years. **Rod Burton**, who owned the agency, was highly regarded in the industry. He was a past president of the **Adcraft Club of Detroit** and he knew his way around the Detroit business track. However, he had recently lost his biggest account, **National Bank of Detroit**. He had not cut back on his staff, hoping to replace the lost account. He held on too long and finally had to close the doors of his ad agency. Mike Marontate made some kind of deal with Rod and as a result, we were given to opportunity to "pitch" the Burton Advertising, Inc. accounts, which were now "up for grabs."

Mike and I pitched for and were awarded the **BPA** (Bowling Proprietors Association of Michigan) account. Due to my background in the restaurant field, we also pitched for and were awarded the **Bonanza Restaurants** account for the Michigan area. I began to feel that I was earning my keep, thanks to this new business. The biggest "plum" was when we were given the chance to pitch for the **Metro Detroit Cadillac Dealers Association**. Detroit is the home of **General Motors** and the **Cadillac Motor Car Division**. Successfully handling that account would give us fantastic visibility with all of GM. We were among some ten or twelve ad agencies vying for the Cadillac dealers' account.

Our meeting with the dealers was scheduled at the **Detroit Athletic Club** (DAC). **Doug Dalgleish** greeted us when we arrived for the meeting. Doug was president of the dealer group. When I introduced myself, he said, "Are you any relation to Toby David?" I said, "Yes, he is my father!" Doug said, "My father and I worked with him when we owned a Nash-Rambler dealership, many years ago. We gave him a car to drive, since he was a TV star. He is a wonderful guy. If you are his son, you must by okay, too." I was thrilled that Doug knew my father. Even better, he liked my dad. As Mike and I made our presentation to the dealer group, I admitted that we had no experience with the auto industry. But I assured the dealers that I was a "quick study" and would work hard to pick up what I had to learn. The Cadillac dealers had Mike and me leave the room so they could discuss our presentation. When they called us back into the room, Doug Dalgleish said, "Ron, we have decided to award you our account. However, due to your lack of auto experience, you will be awarded the account 'on probation' pending your performance." I said, "Thank you, fellas, I promise we won't let you down." Mike and I left the meeting three feet off of the ground. We had just been invited into the powerful automobile business. More importantly, the Metro Detroit Cadillac Dealers Association was the most visible and powerful dealer group in the country. We would be under the microscope with Cadillac Division and General Motors. If we did well, the sky was the limit! To celebrate, Mike leased me a Cadillac DeVille to drive, since I would be handling the dealer account. I had my first meeting with the dealers at Doug Dalgleish's dealership. I came prepared with an agenda and all of the necessary items to be discussed. The meeting went well. Doug Dalgleish said, "Now that's how a meeting should go! You were prepared and you didn't waste our time with small talk or stupid jokes. You are off of probation as of now!"

Making Haste...Quickly!

THE SAYING GOES, "MAKE haste, slowly". But I didn't have
that luxury. I had to dig in and bone up on the automobile
business, and Cadillac in particular, as fast as possible. In addition to learning the automobile "lingo" and specifics of each of
the Cadillac products and their competitors' products, I had to
learn to read the "politics" of the car business.

The Cadillac dealer group was my actual client. However,
Cadillac corporate ruled the dealers and their fate. Additionally,
the Cadillac zone office gave the dealers advertising funds to
add to their own funds, which I used to place and produce
their advertising. So I had to keep the corporation happy
as well as my dealers happy. Often, the corporation wanted
things done their way. The dealers didn't always agree. It
was my responsibility to get the job done and keep everyone
happy. It was often like walking a high wire and often it was
very stressful.

Marontate & Company did not have a creative department.
They did have an art director, but there were no writers or
producers. I was V.P. and account supervisor, but I also had
to be the writer, producer and often the director of all of the
creative work for my accounts. Again, my accounts were the
Bowling Proprietors Association, Bonanza Restaurants, and

the Metro Detroit Cadillac Dealers Association.

To get things started with the Cadillac dealers, I wrote, produced and directed a couple of inexpensive videotaped commercials. They were okay, but not of the quality I wanted to achieve for Cadillac. I quickly changed the advertising name of the dealer group. I wanted to call them, "The Cadillac of Dealers." "The Cadillac of..." had become an American slang phrase that denoted something as the best there was—"The Cadillac of boats," "The Cadillac of watches," and so forth, when referring to something that was the best. The General Motors attorneys refused to let me use the name "The Cadillac of Dealers." They were afraid that they would lose their trademark name, Cadillac. I knew that would not happen, but I had to buckle under their immense pressure. Cadillac had been using the phrase "Gold Key Treatment" when referring to how the dealers treated their customers. Customers also received gold-plated keys to their new Cadillacs. So I named the Detroit Cadillac dealers the "**Cadillac Gold Key Dealers.**"

Cadillac corporate advertising had a reputation for being snooty and boring. Cadillac at this time was far and away the luxury car leader in the world. But their advertising lacked excitement and memorability. I was determined to make the dealer advertising better. Although Cadillac spent huge sums of money in producing their television commercials, the end product didn't live up to the cost. I had to be careful of how I proceeded, but I knew I had to "break the mold" and do something exciting for the Detroit dealer group.

I convinced Doug Dalgleish and the other dealers that we had to spend more money in the production of our television and radio commercials. Then, I went to work. I wrote the lyrics to a new musical jingle for the dealers. The lyrics were as follows:

You did it! You did it!
You worked hard and won.

See your Cadillac Gold Key Dealers...
And be number one!

You made it! You made it!
So, now let it show.
See your Cadillac Gold Key Dealers...
Let everyone know!

Celebrate your success!
Show the world you're the best!
See your Cadillac Gold Key Dealers...
Drive the Cadillac crest!

I hired a very talented jingle writer and musician, **Dan Yessian**, to write the music for the jingle. He orchestrated and recorded the jingle using six singers and a 36-piece orchestra. The jingle turned out great! It was upbeat, compelling and exciting. Just what I had hoped it would be.

I wrote scripts for four 60-second and four 30-second television commercials. I also wrote a 60-second radio commercial. I hired **Ultramedia Productions**, who had offices in Detroit and Los Angeles, to produce the commercials. **Bryant Ewing** was the "boss man" at Ultramedia. They had done a lot of wonderful automotive commercials for local and national use. I stipulated to Bryant that he had to use my friend **Jim O'Dea** as the director and cinematographer for the commercials. We determined that the commercials had to be shot in California, due to the weather restrictions in Detroit.

We flew to Los Angeles and the local Cadillac zone office was kind enough to provide me with the use of a Cadillac Eldorado during my stay in California. This was a "perk" I was to enjoy every time I went out of town to shoot Cadillac commercials.

The first commercial was titled "The Best." We hired **Lawrence Pressman** to be our on-camera spokesperson. You

might not recognize his name, but Larry has appeared in countless feature films and TV films as a featured actor. We filmed "The Best" in a Cadillac dealership in Los Angeles. The second commercial was titled "Pleasant Surprise." We rented the use of a landscape nursery located just off one of the Hollywood freeways. "Pleasant Surprise" featured a woman florist whom we see among thousands of colorful flowers. To our surprise, we could not get on the freeway for hours after we finished filming. There was a huge traffic tie-up that stretched for miles. We later found out that a flatbed truck hauling a Nike Missile had lost its load. The gigantic missile had fallen off the truck and onto the freeway. "Pleasant Surprise" almost turned into a huge "kaboom"! The third commercial was titled "Impossible Dream." It featured a builder on his development work site. He tells us how his dream came true—and how he celebrated his success by buying a Cadillac. The fourth commercial was a composite of all three commercials and featured the jingle as the sound track.

We edited the film commercials in Hollywood and brought them back to Detroit. I called a dealer meeting and played them for the Detroit Cadillac dealers. They loved the whole campaign. Doug Dalgleish was so excited, he said, "We have to show these commercials to corporate right now!" He picked up his phone and called to make an appointment with the Cadillac general manager and his general sales and service manager. He also called Cadillac zone manager **Bill Bowles** and asked him to attend the meeting.

Doug Dalgleish and I arrived at Cadillac headquarters on Clark Street in Detroit, where Cadillac general manager **John Grettenberger** and his general sales and service manager **Brazz Pryor** greeted us. Bill Bowles had already arrived and Cadillac advertising manager **Frank Cadicamo** had been asked by John to attend the meeting, too.

We played the jingle and then ran the TV and radio commercials. John Grettenberger asked us to play everything again, and we did. John said, "Gentlemen, that is a great ad campaign. I wish we had produced it. I'm afraid to ask how much you spent to produce all of that material, but tell me." I told John the total cost for the campaign. It turned out to be less than Cadillac normally spent in producing one 30-second TV commercial. John then said, "I knew I shouldn't have asked! Good work, guys." Then he said to Brazz Pryor, "Brazz, give these guys some extra money to air these commercials. They deserve to be seen as often as possible."

We had scored a home run, right out of the chute. Doug Dalgleish was beaming with pride. I was at a loss for words at our success. Doug threw a big party in his penthouse apartment to show the campaign to all of his friends.

The campaign won top honors in the annual Cadillac dealer advertising competition. We won not only the "**Best Dealer Campaign**" award, but also the "**General Sales & Service Manager**" award, the highest award a dealer campaign can win.

The campaign also won a bronze award in the prestigious **International Film & TV Festival of New York**. We also won the attention of General Motors and every Cadillac dealer group in the country.

A couple of weeks later, I was about to go into a meeting with Cadillac zone manager Bill Bowles. As I waited for the meeting to begin, assistant zone manager **Bob Knapp** came into Bowles' office. He wasn't smiling. He held out a parking ticket and said, "Don't you pay your parking tickets?" I had no idea what he was talking about. He went on, "The zone manager in Los Angeles is very upset that he received an overdue notice for a ticket that was written on one of his vehicles." I took the ticket from Bob and looked at the date. It had been written while I was in Los Angeles, filming. Then it dawned on me. I had followed my friend Jim O'Dea to dinner one night. I pulled up to this charming little restaurant that Jim had suggested. The parking valet greeted me and said, "Our lot is full. But leave your car with me and I'll park it when we have room." When I left the restaurant, the valet pulled my car up and didn't say a word. Obviously, the car had been ticketed on the street, before he had a chance to park it. He was so embarrassed that he couldn't tell me what had happened. He had torn the ticket up and thrown it away. When I told Bob Knapp what had happened, he broke into a smile and said, "I'll tell the L.A. zone manager. Maybe he'll let you use another one of his cars when you are back out there." All's well that ends well. But I'll never go back to that restaurant in Los Angeles again.

The Corporate Game!

I HAD BEEN TOLD that even though my first loyalty was to my dealers, I had to be in good stead with Cadillac corporate. The "Gold Key Dealer" campaign had been a big hit with my dealers and the Cadillac zone manager, Bill Bowles. Bill told me he had a dealer group in Ohio that needed focusing. He asked me if I would like to "pitch" to get the account. I said, "Sure I would, Bill." The account was known as the **Northwest Ohio Cadillac Dealers**. The group was made up of 18 dealers in Northwest Ohio. The group was spread out from Toledo, Ohio, in the north to Findlay, Ohio, to the south and Port Clinton, Ohio, to the east.

Bill Bowles arranged for us to present our credentials to the Ohio dealer group. We had to beat out five or six other ad agencies that were vying for the account. The president of the Ohio group was **John Cooper**. John lived in Port Clinton and his dealership was located there, too. What I hadn't known was that John Cooper had called Doug Dalgleish in Detroit to check me out prior to the presentation. Thankfully, Doug had said only good things about me and our ad agency, Marontate & Company.

We won the Ohio account and I made them "Cadillac Gold Key Dealers," too. The beauty of the Gold Key Dealer identity was that it could apply to any Cadillac dealer group in the country. The Northwest Ohio Cadillac Gold Key Dealers paid a fee to my Detroit dealers for the use of our "Gold Key" TV commercials. We customized the tag endings to reflect the Ohio dealers and their dealership names. John Cooper and I soon became good personal friends as well as business associates. Later, having John in my corner would be more important than I knew.

Things soon changed at the corporate level. Braz Pryor and Bill Bowles were suddenly out. **Peter Gerosa** was in as general sales and service manager. **Tom Patrick** was in as Cadillac zone manager. **Peter Levin** replaced Frank Cadicamo as advertising manager for Cadillac. Doug Dalgleish stepped down as president of the Detroit dealer group and was replaced by **Chuck Crissman**. What I didn't know then was that the corporate "musical chairs" would become a way of life for me. The hard part was learning to make a good impression with each new corporate and dealer group "big shot" as they came into power.

We weathered the changes without any problems and I was still in good stead with the corporation and my dealer groups. The biggest problem facing Cadillac and their dealers was that the Lincoln Town Car had overtaken the Cadillac Brougham. It was shocking at the time. The Cadillac Brougham had outsold the entire Lincoln line of products for years. But Cadillac had let the Brougham slip. And it slipped fast. Cadillac was actually thinking of dropping the Brougham from their product line. It was a sad commentary on what can happen if you blink in the car business. It was time to take off the gloves and get competitive with the Lincoln Town Car before it was, too late.

I wrote a script for a television commercial called "**Bigger.**" I presented the script to the Detroit dealers and Peter Levin, the corporate ad manager. The dealers loved the script because it was competitive. But Peter Levin hated the script. He made the following statement to my dealers, right in front of me. He said, "If I had an agency that presented a script like this to me... I would fire them!" Now that's really putting how you feel on the line! For a moment, I didn't know what to do. Then my dealers spoke up. Chuck Crissman said, "We think the script is great! It is high time we do some advertising with some balls to it! We don't care what you think, Peter. We are producing the commercial with our money, so you don't have any business knocking it." Peter Levin and I were enemies from that moment forward. They say that "he who laughs last, laughs best." I would get my chance later.

Bigger is Better!

CHUCK CRISSMAN DECIDED HE would go with me to Hollywood to produce "Bigger." He knew how important its success would be, considering Peter Levin's attitude about the script. We would be in California for at least a week. We planned to produce "Bigger" and another commercial, called "Caring Dealer." We hired Ultramedia as our production company. Bryant Ewing would be our executive producer. I would be the agency producer. Chuck had no idea what went into a production. He wanted to learn why it cost so much and took so long. The steps to final production include casting, wardrobe, location scouting, props, extras, camera equipment, lighting and pre-production meetings. We had rented the entrance to the **Sheraton Hotel in Universal City** as our setting for "Bigger."

Chuck and I were staying at the **Le Dufy Hote**l in West Hollywood. It was condo apartments that had been turned into a hotel that catered to production people. On the first morning, I was getting ready to take the elevator down to the lobby to meet Chuck. The elevator door opened and to my amazement, **Stan Freeberg** walked out of the elevator. I said out loud, "Stan Freeberg!" He said, "Well, what do you know, somebody recognized me!" And then, he went on his way. Stan Freeberg, in his heyday, wrote and produced some of the funniest comedy record albums and radio commercials ever. You may remember his **St. George and the Dragon** (a takeoff of the TV show *Dragnet*) or his commercials to promote church attendance ("We're all just penciled in!") He was truly a genius and I bumped into him just as his career was diminishing.

Chuck and I went to breakfast before going to our pre-production meeting. We were sitting in a little coffee shop. As I was taking my final sips of coffee, I noticed that a man was sitting by himself in a booth across the way. The man was the famous character actor **Norman Fell**. I got up and went over and introduced myself to him. I told him how much I had enjoyed his work. He played the apartment manager in *The Graduate*, starring **Dustin Hoffman**, **Katharine Ross** and **Anne Bancroft**. He also played the apartment manager on the TV series *Three's Company* starring **John Ritter**, **Suzanne Somers** and **Joyce DeWitt**. He had been in numerous other films and TV shows. He smiled broadly and he told me how pleased he was that I liked his work. It is sad when you think of how many great character actors and actresses get so little recognition for their great work and talents.

We were in our pre-production meeting at the Ultramedia offices in the valley. A woman barged into the meeting and said, in a loud voice, "Who the hell is in my parking place? I want that car moved, right now!" I looked up and saw **Bonnie Franklin**. Bonnie starred, along with **Mackenzie Phillips** and **Valerie Bertinelli**, in the hit TV series *One Day at a Time*. Apparently, her office was right next door to the Ultramedia offices. I raised my hand and said, "It is my car. I'll move it." As I walked with her to where my car was parked, she softened. She said, "I didn't mean to be nasty, but this happens to me every day. I hope you will forgive my yelling." I said, "I don't blame you for being upset. I didn't pay any attention to where I was parking. And by the way, your show is great!" She smiled and waved to me as she went to move her car into the spot I was vacating. This certainly was my day for bumping into stars. Only in Hollywood could this have happened.

That night, Brian Ewing and Jim O'Dea took Chuck Crissman and me to dinner at the **Dar Maghreb** restaurant. It was located on Sunset Boulevard, right across from the S.A.G. (Screen Actors Guild) offices. The restaurant featured North African food. You sat on cushions on the floor and ate the most delicious and unusual food you ever tasted, using bread chunks to scoop your food. The waiters were all at least six-foot-five, wearing a fez and vest and speaking the menu to you. There was no printed menu. There was also a small musical group who played North African sounds as a beautiful belly dancer wiggled her way from table to table. Chuck Crissman spoke to her and learned that she was actually an Irish girl from New York. He asked her if she would like to be an extra in the Cadillac commercial we were filming the next day. I said, "Chuck, we have our cast and our extras. I'm right on budget. She will put us over budget." Chuck said, "I'm the client. I'll take care of it." So the belly dancer was hired.

The next morning, we filmed "Bigger." Our cast was perfect. Especially an actor named **Bud Davis**. His performance really made the commercial "special." In the commercial, two middle-aged, well-dressed couples are leaving the hotel. As they approach the valet, one man says, "My Lincoln Town Car, please." The other man says, "My Cadillac Brougham, please." The Lincoln man says, "Too bad Cadillac doesn't make a big car anymore." Just then, the Lincoln Town Car drives up. "Now that's a really big car!" says the Lincoln man. The Cadillac Brougham drives up and eclipses the Town Car. "Mine's bigger!" says the Cadillac man. The Lincoln man's face drops and he says, "Well, mine's pretty big!" As the Cadillac couple drive off, the Lincoln man says, "I'll have to remember that the next time I buy a **big** car." Everything went well with the shoot. Except that Chuck's "belly dancer" kept complaining that she didn't think she "had to stay here all day!" We all had a good laugh at that one. We were all pleased with how things had gone. That night, Jim O'Dea, Chuck and I went to dinner at the **Ma Maison** restaurant in Beverly Hills. As we entered the restaurant, I noticed that the #1 table was occupied by **Kirk Douglas** and his wife and **Don Rickle**s and his wife. We were seated at the back of the restaurant, facing the front. We could see table #1 from our table. After we ordered a drink, I excused myself to go the men's room. Chuck Crissman said, "I dare you to say something to Don Rickles!" I said, "Okay, just watch me!" I had to walk past their table to get to the men's room. As I passed, I paused and said to Don Rickles, "Good evening, hockey puck!" (Hockey puck is an expression that Rickles uses in his comedy routine.) I kept moving and went to the men's room. As I was returning to our table, Rickles grabbed my arm and said, laughing, "You have some nerve, stealing my lines!" Then, he asked me what I was doing in Hollywood and I told him. He then introduced me to his wife and to Kirk Douglas and his wife. I said hello and I told the Douglas's how much I admired their son Michael's work. I said, "You must be very proud of his accomplishments!" They beamed and said, "Yes, we are very proud of Michael! Thank you for saying so." I returned to our table. Chuck and Jim had witnessed the entire exchange, and Chuck was flabbergasted that I had had the nerve to do what I had done. I said to Chuck, "They're just people. They get into their pants one leg at a time, just like you and me!"

The next day was Saturday. We had to wait until Monday to film "Caring Dealer." Chuck wanted to go to **Rodeo Drive** to do some shopping. I said, "Fine!" We went into **Georgio's**. I was shocked at the prices on their merchandise. But I found a sweater and scarf for my wife that I could afford. Chuck had more shopping to do. So I went over to the bar they have for customers, right in the store. I ordered a drink and stood at the bar while Chuck finished his shopping. There was a large man, wearing starched and pressed coveralls, sitting at a small table near the bar. He was very well groomed and his fingernails were shiny. A beautiful blonde kept coming over to him, complaining, "I can't find anything that I like!" He kept saying, each time, "Damn it! I want you to buy something. Keep looking!" He struck up a conversation with me. I asked him what he did for a living. He said, "I don't really work anymore. I own a country. It is an island, but it is really recognized as a country. I have my own live-in priest, too." If we had been anywhere but in Georgio's, I would not have believed him. There is so much money in Beverly Hills and Hollywood that anything is possible.

Early the next week, we finished our filming and Chuck and I returned to Detroit. The Detroit Cadillac dealers were thrilled with "Bigger" and "Caring Dealer." Both commercials had turned out well. Chuck Crissman insisted that we show the "Bigger" commercial to Peter Gerosa and Peter Levin at Cadillac immediately. Peter Gerosa loved "Bigger." He kept having me run the commercial over and over for him. He turned to Peter Levin and said, "Tell me Peter, why didn't you want Ron to make this commercial?" Peter Levin's face flushed and he said, "I have to admit. They produced the commercial with a lot of class and taste. I guess I was wrong, Pete."

Not only did I have my "last laugh," but "Bigger" created a sensation across the country. Dealer groups representing 400 Cadillac dealers in 36 states bought the rights to run "Bigger" on TV in their marketing areas. Cadillac ran the commercial **seven times** on the national telecast of the **Masters Golf Tournament** on **CBS-TV**. Nationally syndicated cartoonist **Bill Day** drew a cartoon strip with President Reagan and Nikita Khrushchev arguing about who had the "bigger" killer bomb. Articles ran in *Car and Driver* magazine, *Adweek, Fortune* magazine, *Ward's Auto Dealer, Automotive News,* and *Advertising Age.* Newspaper stories appeared in the *Miami Business Herald* and the *Boston Phoenix* and five different articles were written in the ***Detroit Free Press***. The story was also covered by local Detroit TV stations and by ***CNN News*** on cable TV. The best thing that happened was that Cadillac Brougham sales went up 44 percent in Detroit and 17 percent nationwide during the time the commercial was running. Cadillac V.P. and general manager John Grettenberger said, in a letter to Chuck Crissman, "'Bigger' has probably become the best-known commercial in Cadillac's recent history."

I wrote a sequel to "Bigger" called "Lower Cost/ Higher Resale." We flew Bud Davis and the woman who had played his wife in "Bigger" into Detroit and filmed the sequel at one of the Detroit dealers' showrooms. Best of all, Peter Gerosa funded the cost of filming the sequel commercial. Never before had Cadillac corporate given the local dealers a dime towards production costs. In the sequel commercial, the Lincoln man actually goes to a Cadillac showroom to check out the Brougham and the other Cadillac models. He is impressed with the Seville, the DeVille and the Allante. Then he spies the Brougham. He checks the sticker price and is aghast to find that the Brougham costs less than his Town Car. A salesman approaches and he says, "This Brougham costs less than my Town Car." And the salesman says, "Yes, and it has a higher resale value, too!" The Lincoln man is crushed. We dissolve to see him getting into a Brougham for a test drive.

The "Bigger" experience was wonderful. It has to be considered my third "15 minutes of fame."

Riding the Crest

IN ADDITION TO ALL of the press coverage, "Bigger" won a silver medal in the International Film & TV Festival of New York. It also won the award as the "Best Cadillac TV commercial" for that year. To add to it, I called syndicated political cartoonist Bill Day to thank him for doing the "killer bomb" strip. He asked me if I would like to have the original artwork of the cartoon strip. I said, "Yes, I would, thank you!" He sent the original artwork to me with the inscription, "To Ron David. Congratulations on your idea going national!" It was signed "Bill Day, 4/26/87." I have that artwork framed and displayed in my award collection to this day.

The best thing that happened was that since sales of the Cadillac Brougham had risen so sharply, Cadillac decided not to stop production on it. It continued to be produced and sold for another decade or so.

I had become the "fair-haired boy" with Cadillac and the Cadillac dealers. Everything was going well with the dealers and with the corporate people at Cadillac. The dealers asked me to write a competitive commercial, pitting the Cadillac DeVille against the Lincoln Continental. So I wrote a script called, "Quicker." In the commercial, the DeVille is at a stoplight in the left lane. A Lincoln Continental pulls up to the right at the stoplight. The left lane ahead is closed for repairs. The DeVille will have to move into the right lane when it leaves the stoplight, before it reaches the construction area.. The drivers look at each other and the light changes. The DeVille lurches forward, and just before it reaches the construction zone, it moves ahead of the Continental and changes to the right lane. The Cadillac driver looks into his rearview mirror as we see the Lincoln Continental fade into the distance. The voice-over announcer says, "These days, Cadillac drivers are looking at the competition in a whole new way...in their rear-view mirror."

I hired the Ultramedia group to produce the commercial. And again, Jim O'Dea was to be my director/cinematographer. We selected a location in Culver City, California, to shoot the commercial. We had our pre-production meetings at the Ultramedia offices. The drivers for both cars were precision drivers. We had to pay to have policemen and firemen on duty at the shoot. Everything was in readiness.

The weekend came, and Jim O'Dea invited me to spend the day at his house at **Manhattan Beach**. His house was facing an alley. There was another row of houses toward the beach. Jim had a clear view of the beach, because the house across from him had been torn down and a playground had been installed. I asked Jim who put the playground in. He told me that the four-story house to the left of the playground was owned by the widow of the man who invented "the chip" (yes, the famous chip that made computers and so much more possible.). She had bought the house that would have blocked Jim's view of the beach for one million dollars. She had it torn down and had the playground installed, so that her two-year old son would have a place to play! It is hard to fathom having that kind of money, isn't it?

Manhattan Beach is one of several beaches that stretch south to **Redondo Beach**. There is a paved walkway that stretches the entire length of the beaches. People run, roller blade, and bike ride the walkway at all hours of the day and night. The beaches are lined with hundreds of volleyball nets, where hundreds of "hard bodies" play volleyball as you walk along the walkway. Jim played hockey, so he was very good on roller blades. He put his skates on and loaned me his bicycle to ride. We were moving down the walkway when we came to a pier. Jim suddenly told me to stop riding. I got off my bike and followed Jim to the pier. There were two girls sitting on the edge of the pier, with their legs dangling. Jim and I approached them. Jim greeted one of the girls. He said, "How are you doing, Pam?" She said, "Fine, Jim. Who's your friend?" Jim introduced me to **Pam Dawber**. She starred in the TV series ***Mork and Mindy*** with **Robin Williams**. It turns out that Jim and Pam had been neighbors and schoolmates in Bloomfield Hills, Michigan, when they were kids. Jim and Pam had remained friends and kept in touch on a regular basis.

The next day, Sunday, I was on my own. I decided to go to dinner, by myself, at a restaurant in Beverly Hills called **The Gingerbread Man**, which was owned by actor **Carroll O'Connor**. I had dined there before with friends and enjoyed the tuna steak dinner. It was so tender that it literally melted in your mouth! I was seated at a table where I could see Carroll O'Connor sitting, smoking his pipe and talking to a male friend. During my meal, a woman went up to the piano player and started singing a song. She sounded very good. But to my amazement, Carroll O'Connor went up as she finished her song and told her to sit down. She went back to her table, where she was sitting with friends, and broke into tears. I went over to her table and asked her what had happened. She said, "Oh, he hates it when I sing. He lets other people sing. But he won't let me sing." I couldn't let it rest there. I went over to the table where Carroll O'Connor was sitting and I said, "Excuse me, Mr. O'Connor. I am a customer and I liked the way that woman sang. How come you made her stop singing?" O'Connor said to me, "She's a pain in the ass. I don't like her or her voice. Besides, I own this restaurant. I can decide who sings and who doesn't!" I knew it would be futile to argue the case any further, so I said, "Yes, I guess you do have the hammer, Mr. O'Connor. But I don't think you are being fair with that lady." I returned to my table, finished my dinner and left. The real Carroll O'Connor is nothing like the character he played as **Archie Bunker** on *All in the Family*. Nor was he anything like the police chief he played in the TV series *In the Heat of the Night.*. I wish that I could have met him under different circumstances.

That Monday, we filmed "Quicker" on the streets of Culver City. When I returned home, we showed the commercial to our dealers and to the Cadillac people. All were pleased with the commercial. Little did I know that it would be the last commercial I would produce in Hollywood, California.

Larry Anderson, who was merchandising manager for Cadillac, called and asked me if I would like to pitch the Florida Cadillac dealer group. The Florida dealer group, at that time, was the largest-volume dealer group in the country. I told Larry that we would love to have the chance to pitch the group. So he set it up.

Mike Marontate and I flew to Florida and did the pitch to the Florida dealers. That night, we were having dinner together. The next day, I was to return to Detroit. Mike was going to drive to another city in Florida and play golf with a business associate of his. As we were dining, I started on Mike about how he treated his employees. Mike had always treated me well. I think he respected me too much to treat me like he did the rest of his people. I felt that they were underpaid and underappreciated by Mike. I had voiced my feelings to Mike on many occasions. I guess this time was one too many. Mike exploded on me. He said, in a loud voice, "If you don't like the way I treat my employees, that's tough! I am the boss. It's none of your business how I treat them. You're fired!" He dropped his napkin on the table and left the restaurant. I was dumbfounded. It probably wasn't any of my business. But I just can't stand to see people mistreated. I have to speak up.

Actually, Mike did me a great favor that night. I had been told by a Cadillac executive that giant dealer groups were being formed to consolidate and simplify the coordination of certain areas. The new mega-groups would be called CDMAs (Cadillac Dealer Marketing Associations.) My Northwest Ohio dealer group was to become part of a newly formed CDMA called the Central States CDMA. I would either have to pitch to handle the new CDMA or I would lose my Northwest Ohio group when they were absorbed into the new CDMA. I had been concerned that Marontate & Company was too small an ad agency to be considered for the job. Even though I was well thought of by my Northwest Ohio dealers and Cadillac, I could lose out when the change came. The new CDMA encompassed all of the Cadillac dealers in Ohio and West Virginia. Instead of 18 or 19 dealers, there would be 84 dealers in the Central States CDMA. I wanted that group. But I knew I would have to move to a new and bigger ad agency to have a chance. Unwittingly, Mike had just given me that chance.

A couple of days later, Mike returned to the office in Detroit. I followed him into his office. I said, "Mike, did I get it right? Did you fire me the other night at dinner?" Mike said, "Do you want to be fired?" I said, "Wait a minute, Mike. Did you or did you not fire me?" Mike said, "I guess I did." I said, "Fine. I'll pack up and be out of here today!" I called my wife, Cari, to come and get me, since I had to turn in my company car. And that was that. The problem now was to convince my Metro Detroit and my Northwest Ohio dealer groups to follow me to whatever new ad agency I would go to work for. If they didn't want to stay loyal and follow me, then what?

Moving on to the Big Time!

I WAS SUDDENLY A captain without a ship. The first thing I had to do was to determine where I stood with my dealer groups. I called Doug Dalgleish and told him what had happened. I assured him that I would join a bigger and better ad agency. He said he would call all of the Detroit dealers and get back to me. Then I called John Cooper, the president of the Northwest Ohio dealer group, and he also said he would poll the dealers and get back to me. Within a day, both Doug and John called me back, and they both said the same thing: "We will follow you wherever you go!" I was elated. Now, I had to decide which agency I would approach.

There are over 200 ad agencies in Detroit. Any of them would love to have the Cadillac dealer business. But I chose to call Mort Zieve and Jim Michelson at Simons Michelson Zieve Advertising. Perhaps it was because I had such a long track record with them. Going all the way back to WXYZ-TV through Bartlett Film Services, Elias Brothers Big Boy Restaurants, and American Speedy Printing, I had felt comfortable with SMZ Advertising. Mort and Jim were very interested in talking with me. We set up a meeting. I showed them my reel of commercials that I had written and produced for the Cadillac dealers. They were so impressed that they said, "Maybe we should hire you as our creative director!" Instead, I became vice president and account supervisor. The captain had found a ship!

I knew some of the people at SMZ, but I had never met their creative director, Larry Steinberg. After getting settled in my new office, I called a meeting with Larry and his creative staff. I showed them my commercial reel. Then I proposed that I work with them on the creative stuff for Cadillac. After all, my work had won several awards. But to my dismay, Larry Steinberg said, "No, account people don't write for our accounts. You feed us the information and we will do the writing and producing." I should have known then that there would be difficult times ahead.

Within a short time, the call came from Cadillac corporate. We were invited to pitch the new **Central States Cadillac Dealer Marketing Association (CDMA)**. The new group included my Northwest Ohio dealers and all of the rest of the dealers in Ohio and West Virginia. There were 84 dealers in all. The presentation took place in Cincinnati, Ohio. There were eight or ten other ad agencies pitching for the account. Larry Anderson at Cadillac and John Cooper told me that they wanted me to get the new CDMA account. I made the presentation, using the commercials I had already produced for my Cadillac dealers. I know that Larry and John did a lot of talking behind the scenes in my behalf. When my presentation was over, I drove back home and waited for the call. Mort Zieve called me and told me that Larry Anderson had called him and told him that we won the new CDMA account. This meant that we would be handling the fourth-largest Cadillac dealer group in the country, plus the Detroit dealers. We now had 97 Cadillac dealers. I called Doug Dalgleish and told him. He was happy for me. But he said, "I hope that this mega-group doesn't distract you from what you are doing for the Detroit group!" I assured him that my first loyalties would always be with him. He had given me the chance to get into the automobile game in the first place.

The new CDMA along with the Detroit CDMA represented millions of advertising dollars we would be handling and placing. In addition to the dealer funds, Cadillac kicked in tons of additional ad funds, which we also placed. My deal with SMZ gave me a hefty percentage of the commission we would earn with both accounts. My financial future looked brighter than it ever had before.

Leasing had become very important in the car business. Price tags on all cars, especially luxury cars, had skyrocketed. Leasing allowed the car companies to offer affordable monthly leasing fees to customers who could not afford to pay cash or didn't want to borrow big money to drive a new car. To facilitate the leasing information, which changed rapidly, we produced "donut" commercials. A "donut" commercial is one where the beginning and end of the commercial are produced like any other commercial. There is a middle section of the commercial that is changeable to facilitate the leasing deal. So the first assignment I gave to the SMZ creative staff was to develop a "donut" commercial for Cadillac leasing.

The commercial was named "Hot," and it featured bikini-clad women floating around on air mattresses in a swimming pool. I was not happy with the commercial. I knew that the young writers and producers at SMZ really didn't understand the luxury car market. Even worse, they had no idea of the image Cadillac wanted to present in all of their messages. Some of my commercials had "pushed the envelope," so to speak. But "Hot" pushed the envelope to the breaking point. When I presented the "Hot" commercial to my dealers and the Cadillac corporate people, they gave me a "look" that said volumes. However, they approved the commercial for airing. I knew that I had a lot of work to do with the SMZ creative people. And I had to do it fast!

The next ad campaign that SMZ wrote for Cadillac was a series of "donut" commercials. They featured a spokesperson who worked with miniature items that symbolized the point of each commercial. We decided to produce the commercials in Chicago at the **Harpo Studios**. Harpo is Oprah spelled backwards. Harpo Studios is owned by **Oprah Winfrey**. She owns a whole city block of Chicago. Harpo Studios is where she does her syndicated TV show. It also has several large sound stages for film and video production. We filmed for two days at Harpo. During one of the breaks in production, I was invited by the Harpo people to take a tour of the facilities, including the *Oprah* show studio and offices. It was an immense operation. They even had facilities to duplicate each TV show and ship it out to their participating TV stations across the country overnight. We were in the lobby at one point during the tour. There was a dramatic, winding staircase that led to the second floor. As we were ascending the staircase, Oprah was walking down the stairs. She paused as her associate said, "Oprah, I would like you to meet Ron David. He and his people are producing some Cadillac commercials in one of our sound stages." Oprah held out her hand and I shook it. She told me how pleased she was that we had chosen to film our commercials in her studios. We made some additional small talk and she went on her way and so did we. I knew when I met her that I was in the presence of a very special person. She has tremendous charisma and a way of making you feel special, too, when you meet her.

The commercials we produced in Chicago were better than the "Hot" commercial. But they were not the standout quality of the commercials that had preceded them, like "Bigger" and "Quicker." I knew we had to do better.

Even though I was not happy with the creative work the SMZ people were coming up with, I still was considered the "fair-haired boy" by the people at Cadillac corporate. When they formed the Michigan CDMA, we didn't even have to pitch for the business. Larry Anderson called a meeting at SMZ and just gave us the Michigan CDMA account. The Michigan CDMA had 28 dealers. So now with Detroit, Central States, and

Michigan, we were handling the advertising for 125 Cadillac dealers. Cadillac had become the most important piece of business that SMZ handled. The three CDMA accounts kept my assistant, **Karen Cameron**, and me very busy. We drove to meetings all over Detroit, other parts of Michigan, Ohio, and West Virginia.

We handled the load well and got along famously with all of our dealers and with the Cadillac people. Finally, the SMZ creative people came up with a good TV script. It was called "Elevator." We decided to film the commercial in Detroit. I hired Jim O'Dea to act as the production company and to also direct and shoot the commercial. In the commercial, people are getting into an elevator. The elevator has an operator. He calls out the floors as the elevator ascends. When the elevator reaches the second floor he says, "Fourth floor. Mid-sized cars." The doors close, and when they reopen, the operator says, "Top floor. Luxury cars. Cadillac!" A good-looking man leaves the elevator, and we see a beautiful display of Cadillacs for him to admire. We cut back to the elevator. A man says to the operator, "Where are the Lincolns? The operator holds out his arm to protect the passenger as the door closes and he says, "Lincolns?" Going down!" And the elevator door closes. The commercial was very funny. My dealers and the Cadillac folks were very pleased with it. It won the "Best Competitive TV" award that year from Cadillac.

Things went well for several years. But, as with most things in life, there were changes coming. And as with most changes, they would not be for the better.

And Now, the End is Near!

THE TROUBLE BEGAN WHEN the Cadillac national ad agency, **D'Arcy, Masius, Benton & Bowles**, began pressuring Cadillac to let them place the dealer support funds. We had been buying media with those funds for our groups and we got paid a commission for doing so. Cadillac was spending millions of dollars in support of the CDMAs. D'Arcy won out. We now had to do the media planning for the factory support funds. But D'Arcy made the actual "buy" and got the commission. Every regional ad agency in the country had to go through what we were going through. It cost all of us a lot of money. And it wasn't fair. But who ever said dealing with large corporations was fair?

To add insult to injury, Mort and Jim assigned me to a couple of other agency accounts. I was made senior account manager for **Detroit Edison**, the local electric utility company. I had a great gal as my account executive, so I didn't have to spend an undue amount of time on the account. I did get to do a radio commercial with **Joe Dumars**, who at that time was a star basketball player for the **Detroit Pistons**. He now is president and CEO for the Pistons organization. I was also assigned to manage a small group of auto parts stores, **Pronto Auto Parts**. I didn't receive much compensation for the extra duty. It did not make me a happy camper!

The last TV commercial we produced on location was for the Cadillac DeVille. We had a smaller than usual budget for production. So we decided to film the commercial in Scottsdale, Arizona. It was cheaper than filming in Hollywood. I didn't mind, because my father, stepmother, aunt, and a sister lived in Mesa, Arizona, a suburb of Scottsdale. The filming would give me a chance to spend some time with them. We didn't hire Jim O'Dea to direct and film the commercial. Maybe that was bad luck. Who knows? Anyway, the filming went well. And I got to spend some time with my family members. On the last night that I was in Arizona, I had dinner with my father and stepmother at their retirement complex. It was very nice. I didn't know that it would be the last time I would see or talk to my father. Six months later, he was leading a songfest for the retirees and he dropped dead in his tracks. I was grateful that I had the opportunity to be with him one last time.

Cadillac corporate began putting the pressure on the regional ad agencies to do more "direct marketing" on behalf of the CDMAs. They felt that we had to get more "grass-roots" involvement with potential Cadillac customers. So we began developing events where we could sponsor and have "ride 'n drives." We would bring cars to the event and invite patrons to actually drive a Cadillac on a course we would set up near the event. We did all kinds of events. There were golf tournaments, horse jumping shows, polo matches, and even shopping mall events. These events took a great deal of planning and coordination. We didn't make as much on those events as we did on producing commercials and placing media for the Cadillac dealers.

I must admit, the golf tournaments were fun. I got to meet some great golfers, among them **Lee Trevino**, **Sammy Snead**, **Tom Weiskopf**, **Larry Ziegler**, **John Daly**, **Arnold Palmer**, and **Curtis Strange**, just to mention a few. We had a private cocktail party at the event where Arnold Palmer was playing. I had an embarrassing thing happen with Palmer. Years before, when I was handling the Elias Brothers Big Boy Restaurant account, I tied-in on a promotion with the Michigan Arnold Palmer putt-putt courses. I used this experience as an excuse to talk to Arnold Palmer. I walked over to Arnold and struck up a conversation. I related the entire story of the promotion with his putt-putt courses and Elias Brothers. He stared at me through the whole story, and when I finished, he didn't respond. He didn't say one word! I flushed with embarrassment and walked away, upset. What I didn't know was that he had just discovered he had prostate problems, and he was in a lot of pain. I found this out later. So it was easy to forgive him for his apparent snub.

I was at a cocktail party for a charity golf tournament in Youngstown, Ohio. The organizer of the tournament came up to me and said, "Guess who your playing partner is tomorrow, Ron?" I said, "Who is it?" She said, "You are going to play nine holes with **Curtis Strange**! Isn't that great?" I said, "My God, I'm a Sunday duffer. I am sure to be embarrassed." I did play the nine holes with Curtis Strange, though, and he couldn't have been nicer. We talked about family and a lot of other things. He put me completely at ease. I even had a couple of good shots.

I was beginning to tire of all the direct marketing events. They meant a lot of driving and long stretches away from home. But we had no choice in the matter. These events were costly, and I don't believe they sold many cars for Cadillac or the dealers.

My wife, Cari, and I were attending the annual Cadillac Announcement Show. That year, it was being held in Las Vegas, Nevada at one of the big hotels. The entertainment for the final banquet was **Sammy Davis Jr.** He did a fantastic show. The audience was overwhelmed with delight. He wanted to do more, but he told the audience that Cadillac wouldn't let him. What none of us knew at the time was, the next week he would be diagnosed with throat cancer. He never performed again. We had witnessed the last performance ever for a great entertainer... Sammy Davis Jr.

Things went from bad to worse with Cadillac. A top executive with Cadillac was influenced by a competing regional ad agency. They convinced him to pressure the Detroit Cadillac dealers to fire SMZ Advertising and hire them. My friend Doug Dalgleish did everything he could to prevent it from happening. But a couple of the Detroit dealers were swayed by the Cadillac executive, and we lost the Detroit CDMA account. Not long after that, the same guy tried to put us in jeopardy with our big Central States CDMA account. This time, the dealers stuck with us. Again, my friend and client John Cooper and Cadillac merchandising manager Larry Anderson went to bat for us. The dealers ended up telling Cadillac that they would decide who their ad agency was to be, and in so many words, they said, "Butt out! We have no reason to fire SMZ Advertising at this time." So we kept the Central States CDMA account. We also still had the Michigan CDMA account. Cadillac never came after that account.

The final straw with Cadillac came when they told all of the regional ad agencies that they had to stop producing commercials for the dealer groups and use the ads that had been produced by the national ad agency, D'Arcy. Without being involved with the creative materials, every regional ad agency was relegated to being a media buying service, except for the direct marketing efforts. I could see the handwriting on the wall. Cadillac was planning to get rid of all the regional ad agencies and give the dealer ad budgets and control over to their ad agency, D'Arcy, Masius, Benton & Bowles. I didn't know how soon this would happen, but I knew it was coming.

The dealers probably knew it was coming, too. They lost their enthusiasm for advertising when we lost control of the creative. Things were getting tense. My assistant also knew what was coming. One morning I picked her up at the ad agency to drive to a meeting with the Michigan CDMA in

Lansing, Michigan. She was in a foul mood right from the get go. During the meeting, she kept talking to the dealer sitting next to her while I was trying to make a point with the president of the dealer group. I said to her, "Karen, there can only be one meeting going on here!" She stopped talking and I finished the meeting. On the way back to the agency, she was silent. She later went to Mort and Jim and told them that I had caused a "scene" with the Michigan dealers. I told Mort and Jim my side of the story, but I think they chose to believe her. That was the last straw!

I asked Mort Zieve and Jim Michelson to have lunch with me the next day. I went over what had happened in Lansing. I told Mort, whom I had known and worked with for over four decades, "You seem to choose to believe Karen over my word! To tell you the truth, I'm hurt. I would like to make a proposal. I had planned on working another year and a half. But under the circumstances, I don't think I want to now. Why don't you and Jim buy out my interest in the Cadillac business?" They were shocked. But after a minute, Mort said, "Let us put together an agreement and we will get back to you." Within a week, they had an agreement written up and they presented it to me. It was a pretty good deal. I would have a "golden parachute" of income and health insurance that would last until Social Security payments kicked in for me. I also got to keep the Cadillac DeVille for a few more months, until the current lease ran out.

I accepted their offer. And a career that spanned over forty-five years came to an end!

Epilogue

THANKSGIVING 1997 HAD SPECIAL meaning for my family and me. It was the first day of my retirement. Turkey never tasted so good!

My retirement has not been what you might expect. I am busier now than when I was working, it seems. I had a business on the Internet for a year. I am vice chairman of the board, chairman of the fund-raising committee and a volunteer reader for the Michigan Chapter of Recording for The Blind & Dyslexic. We record books onto CDs to help visually impaired students from first grade through grad school get their education. I play the piano, golf, bowl, and read. Too often, there doesn't seem to be enough time in the day to get it all in.

I was born prematurely, under five pounds. The first seven or eight years of my life were tough. I had pneumonia three times before I was five. Every childhood malady that you could imagine came my way. Measles, mumps, chickenpox, whooping cough, you name it. I had them all. My mother got divorced twice. I had two failed marriages. The third one, thank God, was worth it. I have been married to my wonderful Cari for over twenty-five years. All were wonderful years.

When I walked into WXYZ-TV on that first day in 1952, I had no idea what was ahead. My career took me in many directions. Happily, the only time I was ever out of a job was at my own discretion. I had a lot of help along the way, especially during those early days. I have been blessed with many people who believed in me and in my talent.

I have had the opportunity to work with and meet hundreds of talented and famous people. There were even more than I have recounted at this writing.

From the early "pioneering" days of television through the "digital age" of editing and recording, a lot has happened. I learned a lot and hopefully, along the way, I taught a few young people some things.

My career was a great ride. I loved every minute of it. God has blessed me with so many wonderful experiences. Yet despite all of the great things that have come my way, I have one regret. I met Bob Hope, Jack Lemmon, Joan Rivers, Rodney Dangerfield, and many others.

But I never met Sinatra!